T0113898

HAVE SOMETHING

TO SPILL

*Ten–Minute Devotions from 1 and 2 Peter,
Along with Survival Tips, Recipes, and
Inspiration for the Moms of Littles*

KARA E. EDWARDS

WESTBOW
PRESS®
A DIVISION OF THOMAS NELSON
& ZONDERVAN

WestBow Press books may be ordered through booksellers or by contacting:

WestBow Press
A Division of Thomas Nelson & Zondervan
1663 Liberty Drive
Bloomington, IN 47403
www.westbowpress.com
844-714-3454

Scripture quotations are from the ESV® Bible (The Holy Bible, English Standard Version®), copyright © 2001 by Crossway, a publishing ministry of Good News Publishers. Used by permission. All rights reserved.

ISBN: 978-1-6642-4755-0 (sc)
ISBN: 978-1-6642-4756-7 (e)

Library of Congress Control Number: 2021921224

Print information available on the last page.

WestBow Press rev. date: 11/11/2021

Beloved husband,

Thank you for believing and investing in me. It is an honor and a joy to do life alongside you. We make a good team. Our kiddos adore their daddy, and I couldn't be more grateful. Thank you for teaching me so much as my pastor and for supporting me as my best friend. I love you always and forever.

My amazing kiddos,

I say this often, but I truly do love being your momma. You are incredible gifts. It is such a privilege to get to spend my days with you, watching you grow, learn, and enjoy life. I'm excited to see God's plans for you unfold. I love each of you with everything in me—always.

Love, Momma

Mom and Dad,

Thank you for your patient love, faithful prayers, wise guidance, and proactive teaching. You taught me to love Jesus first, serve others well, and always be my husband's biggest fan and our children's loudest cheerleader. You have always supported and encouraged my dreams. Thank you. Love you both bushels.

DEAR PRECIOUS MOMMA HOLDING THIS BOOK

I'm so excited to begin this journey with you. Motherhood is tough, amazing, overwhelming, and beautiful. Know that you are not alone.

Before you begin this unique devotional, here are a few quick tips.

1. Grab a Bible.

I highly encourage you to use a tangible Bible because it feels most personal, but if you use an app or Google to look up the verse, that's okay, too. The important thing is that you are reading God's Word—His voice to us. If you do choose to use a paper copy, feel free to color, highlight, or take notes in it. Make it personal and a reminder of what you have learned while studying.

2. We Will Journey through 1 and 2 Peter Verse by Verse

First Peter is full of hope and encouragement. Second Peter is not often featured in short Bible studies, but you will be challenged and given meat to chew on. Through both books (letters) you will receive rich and thought-provoking teachings because I know that there are adorable children who need their mommas' cups to be filled. Just because you are a mom of littles with limited time doesn't mean you can't grow in spiritual truth and wisdom during this challenging season. When our cup gets bumped during stressful moments, I want us to be so full of His Spirit and truth that His goodness spills out of us.

3. Plan on Five to Ten Minutes a Day

Seriously, that's it. These devotions are guilt free because they will only take a few minutes of your precious time, but they are *full* of meat and not fluff. There is no more feeling guilty because you haven't completed all of the Bible study homework or spent an hour in the Word each morning. A seminary professor once told me that there will be seasons of motherhood where you can only handle one verse a day (reading it while locked in the bathroom), and that's okay. God is not any more or less pleased with you. There is no guilt. Let's just grow and learn together.

Included after each daily devotion is a fun activity for little ones, encouragement for your marriage and parenting, or a survival tip to use as you face the daily grind. I have not included these because I have mastered parenthood and marriage. You may still find me dealing with a toddler meltdown on aisle five at Walmart or looking grumpy and frumpy while refueling at the gas station. These are, however, just some of the things that I have learned and am still learning during this journey.

You are a gift to your family, and I truly believe that as your cup is filled with the Word of God and His Spirit, what flows out of you when you get bumped along the way will be a foundation and an example for your children to stand on for generations to come. That is my prayer and goal for both of us.

Thank you for joining me on this journey.

Love, Kara

DAY 1

Heavenly Father,

Please use this time to bring me closer to you, fill my cup so it runs over with your Spirit, open my heart, and clear my mind to receive your truth. Please quiet the noise around me. Amen.

TODAY'S READING

1 Peter 1:3–7

1. Who causes us to be born again? Where does salvation come from? (verse 3)

2. If we have a relationship with Him, we have an inheritance that is what? (verse 4)

3. Wow! Don't you feel so much more hope when you know what is waiting for you? The hope that he refers to isn't just wishful thinking. It is a confident expectation.

4. Verse 6 acknowledges the various trials that we face. They are hard, they hurt, and they seem unfair. Why do we have to go through them? (verse 7)

5. What's the result? (verse 7 again) Let's do that.

Gracious Lord,

We praise you for our salvation and the testing and building of our faith. Please soften our hearts and give us grace so that we can cry out to you in sorrow for our sin and for the faith to believe. You are mighty to save. Thank you for sending Jesus to die on the cross for our sins and the new life we can have in Him. Thank you for the living hope we have in you because you are our resurrection and our life. We can face work, a messy house, tired and whiny kids, sleepless nights, broken relationships, sickness, and uncertainty with hope because of your love for us. You offer compassion, friendship, provision, and promises that we can count on. Thank you also for the inheritance that is waiting for us in heaven. It's real, and it's with you. Please fill us with your spirit and strength as we face today's trials with hope. May our faith prove to be more precious than gold when it is tested by fires, today and always. Thank you, Jesus. Amen.

Survival Tip #1

Pray

On good days, pray. On bad days, pray.

Pray without ceasing. (1 Thessalonians 5:17)

Out loud, silently, in a prayer journal, with your kids, with your husband, or with your best friend, pray, pray, and pray. My mom, Karla, taught me this early in my life. Since the age of seven, I've kept a prayer journal. My momma is an excellent Bible teacher, caregiver, cook, gardener, and avid reader, but most of all, I would characterize her as a beautiful prayer warrior. She prays with conviction, passion, and love, day and night.

One day, I was worried about her continually waking at 3:00 a.m., and she simply told me that it was her nightly prayer shift. The Lord had laid it on her heart to pray for specific people at that time. I'm forever grateful for her teaching and example. She longs for people to know and freely speak to Jesus. I love to hear her pray.

Sometimes, my prayers are long, thorough, and for everyone and everything I can think of. Other times, my prayers are as short and simple as this: "Help me, Lord" (That one usually comes on a Monday morning).

God wants a relationship with us. He wants our honesty. Tell Him anything. He can handle it. Thank Him for your blessings, praise Him for being so awesome, pray for forgiveness of specific sins, and pray for the things that you desire or are worrying you. He cares, and He will never leave you. He is faithful and listening.

What I Pray for Our Children

- For them to know, love, and cherish the Lord
- For protection spiritually, emotionally, physically, and mentally
- For them to have teachable hearts
- For anything they are struggling to learn or any way they are hurting
- For them to feel peace, love, and acceptance in our home
- For them to cling to Jesus and trust He is good when their circumstances are not good
- For faith and courage when they are afraid
- For them to always love each other and others well
- For their ambitions and roles in the Kingdom of Christ
- For their future spouses

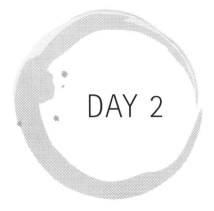

DAY 2

TODAY'S READING

1 Peter 1:6–9

In these verses, Peter acknowledged that we couldn't see God. This is where faith comes in.

1. In what ways do you see God in creation?

2. Have you ever seen God working in your life, answering prayers, or bringing good from something that you never thought was possible? I call those faith builders or jewels from God. If you have extra time today, write down a few of those things as reminders of His goodness.

Even though we can't physically see Him yet, God gives us faith. In return, we are filled with inexpressible joy. Wow. We can be happy and have peace in the midst of our daily circumstances and struggles because of God. God is with us, is for us, and fills us with great hope.

Joy can be so hard to have. Some people who are close to me have battled depression. I used to think that I had to fake happiness to be joyful. The joy that Peter talked about comes from a deep happiness and contentment in the Lord, which comes from our salvation (relationship with Him). I know that when I turn to extra doughnuts, wine, shopping, and Facebook time, I'm not left with a feeling of contentment or deep happiness. However, like this morning, I can wake up feeling empty, grumpy because the sun isn't shining, super tired from interrupted sleep, burdened from sad news, and worried about a friend. But when I take ten minutes to drink my coffee, journal, and read the Bible, I feel my heart shift. I have often asked Him to change my attitude, and He faithfully does every time. His arms are open, and He wants the real, messy, discouraged, and broken us. He can handle anything we lay at His feet.

Blended Cereal Sand

Supply List

- cereal
- blender
- storage container with a lid
- trucks, cars, plastic dolls, dinosaurs, measuring cups, and plastic spoons

Instructions

1. Blend the cereal, stirring occasionally.

2. Pour blended mixture into container.

3. Add toys and other objects.

4. Call your children in and let their imaginations soar.

When playtime is finished, simply store it in the container with a lid on so as not to attract unwanted visitors (mice). Bring it out for daily fun.

Tips

- Supervise your children so that you know the cereal is staying in or near the container.
- Simply sweep up the surrounding mess and pour it back into the container.
- Lay towels down, fill a bowl with soapy water, and allow your children to wash their "sandy" toys. Then lay them out to dry.

  Never shy away from messy play. As the mess grows, so does the imagination.
  —Me, a very messy (and imaginative) mom

DAY 3

TODAY'S READING

1 Peter 1:10–13

1. Verse 10 says, "Concerning this salvation." What exactly is salvation? Salvation is not a matter of trying hard enough or just believing God hears your prayers. God saved me from my sin and ugliness by the blood of Jesus, when He suffered and died. By His grace, I was offered salvation. He changed my heart so that I could feel sorrow for my sin, ask for forgiveness, and receive His mercy. We can't do enough good deeds to earn salvation. If you haven't experienced salvation, cry out to God for forgiveness and faith. Titus 3:5 says, "He saved us, not because of the righteous things we had done, but because of His mercy."

2. As the Spirit led them, the prophets wrote the things that were going to happen, which became part of the Old Testament. They told us that Christ would come and suffer in our place. Christ is in all scripture and not only the New Testament. The Holy Spirit helped them see that they were writing it not only for themselves but also for the future church—us.

3. In verse 13, what does the word *therefore* mean? What is it there for? That's always a good question when reading scripture. The answer is because Christ suffered, the prophets were faithful, were obedient, and wrote it all down for us, and we can understand scripture by the power of the Holy Spirit—*therefore,* we need to prepare for action. We are not just moms, wives, or whatever your job title is. We are set apart and called to live differently—not by our own strength but with our hope.

Where should we set all of our hope? Verse 13 says that we set it fully on the grace that we will receive. We already have a measure of grace that is for our salvation. When Jesus is revealed, we will receive grace in its fullness. As followers who are saved by grace, we will live eternally with Christ. There will be no more sorrow, pain, abandonment, brokenness, awkwardness, stress, feeling left out because we are different from this world, death, sickness, or wondering if we are measuring up. Christ paid it all. So now we actively wait with hope and sober minds set on Christ.

Father,

We thank you for the prophets, that they listened to your Spirit, and that they wrote down the things that would happen, which would further prove the truth of your Word. Thank you for salvation. Thank you that it is a gift that cannot be earned. We thank you for your grace and the hope we have been given.

Please help us to be filled with your Spirit. Help us to hunger for your Word and make it a priority in our lives. We pray that as a result, we will have sober minds fixed on you and unshakeable in this world. May our children see you in us.

You are loving, gracious, mighty, and unshakeable. We give you today and all that we are and need to do. We love you. Amen.

Survival Tip #2

Turn up the Music

The quickest way to change the atmosphere in a home is to turn up the music, especially worship music. I have found that it is super hard to be grumpy when you are praising Jesus. Soon your heart is at ease, the kids are smiling, and a toe begins to tap. Dance parties are the *best*. I also believe that there is great spiritual significance in playing worship music that fills the air. Satan doesn't like it, and he knows he isn't welcome when music that honors Christ comes on.

For we do not wrestle against flesh and blood, but against the rulers, against the authorities, against the cosmic powers over this present darkness, against the spiritual forces of evil in the heavenly places. (Ephesians 6:12)

My Current Playlist

- "Joy of the Lord" (Rend Collective)
- "You Are for Me" (Kari Jobe)
- "Waymaker" (Michael W. Smith)
- "Happy Dance" (MercyMe)

- "Everywhere I Go" (Tim Timmons)
- "It Is Well" (Bethel Music)
- "Break Every Chain" (Jesus Culture)
- "You Will Never Run" (Rend Collective)
- "Brokenness Aside" (All Sons & Daughters)
- "Counting Every Blessing" (Rend Collective)

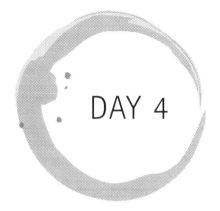

DAY 4

Father,

Please open our hearts and minds to your Word. May your Spirit fill and lead us as we hear from you. Amen.

TODAY'S READING

1 Peter 1:14–21

1. As mothers, we often deal with obedient and disobedient children. However, how often do we think about our own disobedience as children of God?

2. Let's look at verse 14. What are we called to be? I sometimes have a hard time seeing my own sin. I rationalize it instead of repenting of it. I'm quick to see everyone else's sin. Today, let's ask God to show us our sin so that we can repent (turn away and stop) of it and ask for His forgiveness.

3. Are we helping our children see their sins when we ask them to obey? Are we helping them find the heart of the issue (ungratefulness, selfishness, deceit, anger, etc.) and not only focusing on their behaviors?

4. Praise God for the precious blood of Christ. His sacrifice was planned before the foundation of the world was created. It wasn't a plan B because Adam and Eve sinned (see verse 20). Because He was raised from the dead, our faith and hope are in God and not this world. Hallelujah (see verse 21). By God's grace, love, and forgiveness we are made holy and righteous. He wants to help us obey just like we help our children obey. I'm so thankful that I'm not in this alone.

Jesus,

Thank you for faith. We know faith is a gift from you. When our faith wavers, please strengthen it. When doubt creeps in, please renew our faith. Thank you for salvation. Thank you for a relationship with you. Thank you for the forgiveness of sins and helping us to repent and obey you. The joy we can have every day builds our faith, and it is a witness to others. Thank you that you love us so much, you care about us being happy.

Joy in you brings peace, which is lasting and not temporary. We don't have to overindulge in the pleasures of this world to find happiness. It comes from you, and it is a result of your saving grace. We experience it when we turn to you, personally and directly and surrender our lives to you.

Thank you, Jesus. May our spouses, kids, and coworkers see your peace and joy overflowing from our cups when our cups are shaken. Amen.

Pick-Me-Up Iced Coffee

Ingredients

- 2 cups of your favorite coffee
- blender
- 3 tablespoons of sweetened condensed milk
- handful of ice

Preparation

1. Prepare coffee and pour into blender.
2. Add sweetened-condensed milk.
3. Toss in ice.
4. Blend it.

Enjoy this cold deliciousness in your favorite glass or mason jar, and add a straw to make it feel fancy.

Jesus always. Coffee daily.

The Pastor's Perfect Pancakes

When Daddy fixes the pancakes, the kids get super excited. Here's his very own packed-full-of-goodness recipe.

Ingredients

- your favorite pancake batter mix or ingredients
- 1/4 cup oatmeal
- 1/4 cup cornmeal
- 1 egg
- 1/2 cup milk
- 1 teaspoon of vanilla
- cinnamon
- nutmeg

Preparation

Mix pancake batter. Then add oatmeal, cornmeal, egg, milk, and vanilla. Sprinkle with cinnamon and nutmeg. Make pancakes. Serve with strawberries and whipped cream or shape them into Mickey Mouse heads and add M&M's for the eyes and nose and a piece of bacon for the smile. Drizzle with syrup.

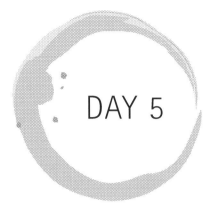

DAY 5

TODAY'S READING

1 Peter 1:22–25

1. How can we love one another with a pure heart? Our culture wants us to think that love and truth are opposites. How can we actively show love to others and even those whom we disagree with?

2. Verse 24 is so humbling to me. It is a great reminder to spend more time being concerned with my spiritual state than with my body. My flesh will get sick, let me down, never look the way that I want it to, and die. It will fade like the grass. However, the Word of the Lord remains *forever*. Our spirits live eternally. How's your spirit today? I'm so encouraged by your faithfulness to study and know the Word of the Lord and make it the priority of your life. God's word brings healing, contentment, and hope. It is the good news—the gospel.

Father,

Thank you for the five days we have spent studying your Word. Please fill our cups with hope and peace, even in our everyday circumstances. May our cups run over into our parenting, marriages, churches, and communities. Please strengthen us, fill us with wisdom, and help us to love others as you love us. In Jesus' name, we pray this. Amen.

Survival Tip #3

Stay Connected

Motherhood can feel isolating. There are several ways to connect with other adults without draining your emotions or thought tank. We all know that those are already running low. Here are a few ideas:

- Text your husband a simple, "I love you. Thanks for all you do." Send him funny stories about your day or frustrating moments that you experienced with the kids. Be friends and comrades on this parenting road.
- Randomly check in with a friend and ask how she is doing. Offer to meet up or invite her over, even if the house is a mess. My treasure of a friend and fellow momma of three, Katie, is so good about doing this for me. She keeps me social, and she has been so patient and consistent in my season of littles. She has also been a faithful comrade in our mom's group, and it has been a joy to grow in faith together. She is a jewel.
- Text pictures of your kids to your husband, parents, siblings and friends. They want to stay connected to you and your children too.
- Leave little notes in the bathroom for your husband and children to find. My parents set the example of doing this, and it is such an encouraging way to begin the day. Someone told me that she remembers seeing the notes my parents left for each other when she was playing at my house as a little girl and thinking, "I want a marriage like that when I grow up."
- Find a loving church and small group. Churches are made up of imperfect people, but it's important on your spiritual journey, to engage with others who are growing and learning just like you.
- Show up at the park and speak to the other moms there. Chances are that one of the moms will feel just like you do.
- If you are feeling super lonely, sign your kids up for an activity just so you can get to know other moms.

When invited, say yes and do it. You'll be glad that you did.

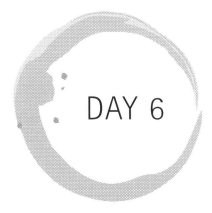

DAY 6

TODAY'S READING

1 Peter 2:1–3

1. This passage starts with the word *therefore*, so as always, we have to ask, "What is the therefore *there* for?" Let's look at the scripture just before it.

2. Peter just finished walking us through salvation, new birth in Christ, and purifying ourselves by obeying the truth so that we can show sincere love. Now in Chapter 2, he asked us to rid ourselves of several sins. How do we do that? We do it by obeying the truth.

3. Having now been reborn, we are to crave spiritual milk, just like a newborn craves the breast or bottle. What is our spiritual milk? Where does it come from? Our spiritual milk is the Word of God. Feasting on it brings growth, strength to flee sin and temptation, and lasting satisfaction. It quenches our thirsts and matures our faith.

4. The Lord is good. We can taste His goodness and crave more. Are you craving more? On the days or in seasons when you aren't craving His goodness, don't be afraid to ask Him to change your desires and increase your longing for Him.

Lord Jesus,

Thank you for another day to praise, worship, and serve you. Thank you for our families and your goodness. Thank you that you have given us your Word, grace, and forgiveness.

Please forgive us for being envious of other women and people, any unkindness and slander that we have shown to others, the deceit and pride that have crept in, and any hypocrisy in our lives. Please convict us and grant us repentance.

I pray that when we fill our kids' sippy cups, bottles, or glasses with milk, they ask for snacks for the millionth time, or we prepare meals for our families, we will take a second to thank you for your Word, which satisfies and tastes good. I pray that we would crave your Word and know that we cannot live spiritually without it. We cannot thrive without it, just like a baby can't thrive without nourishment. Please mature us and fill our cups so that when they spill over this week, our families, friends, coworkers, and even the strangers that we meet will be splashed with your goodness. Amen.

Our Favorite Homemade Playdough Recipes

We have tried many recipes and measured them as precisely as we could; however, they still needed more water, flour, or something. So, without further ado, here are our favorites. It's okay if you need to add more water if it's too dry or more flour if it's too wet. Consider it an experiment.

Baby Lotion Dough
Ingredients

- 1 bottle of baby lotion (any scent or brand is just fine
- 2 C flour

Preparation

1. Pour the bottle of baby lotion into a large bowl.

2. Add flour little by little until the dough is at your preferred texture.

When ready, you can make shapes and pretend to bake them. Use safe kitchen utensils. For example, potato mashers make great stampers.

Salt Dough

Ingredients

- 1 cup salt
- 1 cup water
- 2 cups flour

Preparation

Stir it. Shape it. Bake it.

To bake your shapes, simply place them on a cookie sheet and in a 150-degree oven. Turn them frequently. Bake time varies depending on the size of your shapes.

The Real-Deal Dough

This one is a little more extensive, and it only happens at our house *if* I have all the ingredients on hand. This one does last longer though if you store it in resealable baggies.

Ingredients

- 2 cups flour
- 3/4 cup salt
- 4 teaspoons cream of tartar
- 2 cups water
- 2 tablespoons oil
- food coloring

Preparation

Dump the ingredients into a large bowl. Stir it. Shape it. Play restaurant. Soak up the moment.

DAY 7

1 Peter 2:4–8

1. The true church is God's people. It doesn't matter where you are from or how long you've been a Christian. If you believe the Cornerstone (Jesus) is precious, you are part of the spiritual stones of the church. He was rejected by men but chosen and precious to God.

2. What happens if we trust in Him? (see verse 6) We will never be put to shame. There's no shame at the cross. Jesus took all of our shame, and we get to live with conviction but without shame. We are loved, forgiven, and free.

3. Those who do not believe do not have that same hope. They stumble and fall when they encounter the Living Stone (Jesus) because they do not trust Him. Instead, it says that they disobey the message. In other words, they refuse to believe the gospel and are blind to it (see verse 8).

Father,

Thank you for Jesus, our Living Stone. Thank you for building your church and including us as your spiritual stones. May we give you glory and serve your church well by loving and accepting one another, even if their stones' shapes are different than ours are. Lord, please help us to teach, love, and train our children to be spiritual stones for the church. We also know many who are not saved, do not put their trust in you, or have no relationship with you. Please open their eyes, speak to their hard hearts, and help them to see you—our Living Stone. Thank you, Jesus. Amen.

Survival Tip #4

Keep Baby Wipes Everywhere

Being stranded with a dirty diaper and no baby wipes is not for the faint of heart. I have had to improvise only a couple of times, and it was enough to make me buy them in bulk and never leave a store without them. Baby wipes are priceless.

Here are a few places to keep them.

- Keep a pack in your car for dirty faces, hands, feet, bottoms, car seats, shoes, sunglasses, dashboards, and steering wheels.
- Keep a pack in your purse for all of the above as well as restaurant tables, high chairs, your shirt, your pants, your purse, shopping carts, and juicy sucker faces during church.
- Keep a pack in the bathroom for potty training, toothpaste messes, removing your makeup, "chocolate" on the toilet seat, and to quickly clean when company pulls into the driveway.
- Keep a pack in the garage for sticky Popsicle faces and fingers, outdoor runny noses, emergency potty situations in the yard, wiping off swings covered in bird mess, and killing spiders on slides.
- Keep a pack under the sink so that your kids can dust with them or wipe windows, doorknobs, cabinet doors, and more with them. They are harmless.
- Keep a pack at your mom's house, babysitter's house, the church nursery, the office, and any other place that you frequently go. You just never know when you will need one.

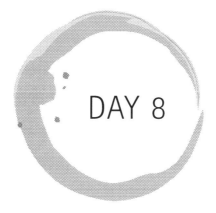

DAY 8

TODAY'S READING

1 Peter 2:9–12

1. What did He call us in Verse 9? He called us chosen, a royal priesthood, a holy nation, a people belonging to God—wowzers! We are His people. Once we weren't His people, *but* Jesus came and changed everything. True believers have now been grafted into the family of God.

2. How did this happen? It happened through His mercy alone. We are chosen not by birthright nor by following all the rules but by His mercy and grace. He changes our heart and calls us, and we respond through repentance and faith.

3. Why? Is it so that we can boast and be better than everyone else or be perfect and have it all together? Nope. The last half of verse 9 says it is so that we may declare His praises. Have you declared them lately? I encourage you to write praises to Him in your journal. Also, I challenge you to turn on some Christian music, dance, and praise Him in front of your kids today. Let them see your hope and joy. You may look silly (I do), but they will always remember their momma praising Jesus.

4. What's next? How do we look different from the other women in the world who are not of a royal priesthood? What good deeds can others see in us that will hopefully lead them to glorify God? (see verse 11)

Father,

Thank you for choosing us because of your great mercy. Thank you for bringing us into your family so that we may glorify and praise you. I pray that we will believe and love differently because of this truth. I pray that others will see the way that we love our husbands, the way in which we parent our children, the way we serve others, and the joy we have and glorify you.

May our hearts be pure. May we not want the glory for ourselves but do things with the intention of you receiving all the glory. We may have a lot of lies and names written on our hearts that others have said about us or we have said about ourselves. Please heal our wounds and help us to see ourselves as you do. We belong to you, and we are loved and cherished. May we look forward with great expectation and excitement to the day when you will visit us. Our hope is in you. Amen.

Family Traditions

We began our own family traditions with our kids at an early age, and I'm so glad we did. They already feel a sense of stability and security within our family. They love having fun things to look forward to that make our days special. It also greatly helps my meal-planning and grocery lists.

Here are a few of the Edwards family's favorite traditions:

- Sunday-night pancakes (Dad cooks!)
- Taco Tuesday
- Friday is movie and pizza night (Our kids get so upset if we miss this night. See the pizza-making tips below.)
- last-day-of-summer-vacation PJ's day (We stay in our PPJ's all day and eat our favorite snacks.)
- treating our neighbors on Halloween (We make treats and deliver them to our neighbors. My mom taught me this when we were little. I've always loved this fun twist on an awkward holiday.)
- attending Christmas Eve service with our church family and then driving around to look at the lights.
- reading the account of the birth of Christ before opening presents on Christmas morning (This is a multigenerational tradition in the Edwards family.)
- making snow ice cream the first time we have enough snow (Get a bowl of fresh white snow. Add 1 teaspoon of vanilla, a little milk, and sugar. Then stir.)
- planting seeds in egg cartons on the first day of spring

My mother-in-law, Vickie, is a very creative and talented quilter and an excellent cook. Most importantly, she raised my husband to know and follow Jesus. She also taught me the following brilliant pizza tips.

1. A sliced English muffin makes a quick child-size pizza crust. Mix tomato sauce and hamburger together, spread it onto the muffin, and then top it with shredded cheese. Pop it into the oven at 400 degrees for 10 minutes. It's a great snack for adults, too.

2. Save your aluminum pie pans. They are the perfect size for make-your-own-pizza night. Let the kids pat out the dough and add their toppings.

DAY 9

TODAY'S READING

1 Peter 2:13–17

1. How can we submit to the government that has been placed in authority over us "for the Lord's sake"? We may have differing opinions on this and be of different political parties, and that's okay. The Bible doesn't say that you have to be of one or the other in order to be a Christian. It does say to submit to and respect authority. I believe that we can do this by following the laws of the land.

When we do good, we can silence foolish people. Doing good is a good testimony for Christ, to our faith, and to our families (see verse 15). It silences others who would speak against us (in many cases).

2. What if the laws of the land go against scripture? Verse 16 says that we are to live free. This isn't a license to sin, but it is a reminder to not fear the government either. We are to live as a servant of God. He is our ultimate authority. He gets the final say in our lives. We fear Him above all else. This is foundational and an important worldview to pass onto our children and their children. The days are coming when our country may look less and less like a Christian nation. Today we are training arrows.

3. In verse 17, we find four powerful commands to build our homes on. How can we better honor everyone inside and outside of our homes? How can we better love our brothers and sisters in Christ? Are we living in ways that show we fear God above all else? How can we better honor our president and leaders?

Lord,

We lift up our president and leaders. We ask that you do a mighty work in their hearts and lives and bring them to a saving faith in you, if they do not already know you as Lord and Savior. Please use them for your glory. Please have mercy on our nation.

Father, please protect our brothers and sisters in the church and please help us to honor our leaders, our country, and one another and love our church family well. We need each other in these uncertain times.

I pray that we won't live in fear, we will live in faith, and we will train our children to have a worldview that is based on your Word. Please help us teach your Word to our children, model it in our homes, and educate them in ways that train them for the many situations and battles that lie ahead of them. We pray that our children will be smart, courageous, and wise arrows for your kingdom. Amen.

Survival Tip #5

Laugh Freely and Often

One night after a stress-filled and weary few weeks, I sat on the couch and read an author's account of her latest embarrassing moment. It started as a giggle, and then I soon broke into hysterical sobs of laughter. My husband thought I had lost my mind. It was a beautiful moment. My heart felt lighter, and my spirit was at ease. Laughter is a gift and a grace from God. I come from a family of laughter, and I have seen firsthand how healing laughter can be.

My dear friend Annie is a missionary and the mother of two sweet girls. She suffers from an autoimmune disease, which has left her with severe chronic pain. However, it hasn't kept her from the mission field. She is brave and bold. Every time I have a conversation with her, I feel like I have met with Jesus. Scripture and love for our Lord flow from her lips. Do you know what else flows from her? Laughter flows from her. She laughs freely and often and expresses her enjoyment of life, even when it physically hurts to do so. I have rarely seen Annie without a smile. In Proverbs 31 where it says that she laughs without fear of the future, that's Annie.

Here are some ways to cultivate laughter in your being and your home.

- Read a lighthearted, humorous book just for fun.
- Watch a comedy.
- Tickle your kids.
- Allow yourself to laugh out loud at memes.
- Share or create an inside joke with your husband.

- Tease each other lovingly and show your children how to receive a harmless joke or friendly teasing.
- Learn to laugh at yourself when you make a mistake or mess.

A Joke for Mom

When my kids become wild and unruly, I use a nice, safe playpen. When they're finished, I come out.
—Erma Bombeck

A Joke for the Kids

Question: What did the momma cow say to her baby?

Answer: It's pasture bedtime.

DAY 10

TODAY'S READING

1 Peter 2:18–25

1. It feels like this passage begins with a little lecture on respecting your boss and then turns to the profound truth of the gospel. Have you ever had a less-than-terrific boss? Have you had a boss who wasn't very respectful but demanded your respect? Have you been in any situation where it would be so tempting to treat that person as poorly as he or she treated you?

2. Here, Peter taught that it is far better for us to suffer unjustly and endure than to sin against others. He wasn't asking us to stay in an abusive situation or an unhealthy workplace or relationship. He was simply pointing out the things that Jesus had endured on the cross. He never sinned, and yet, He was crucified, and it was all for us. If He can go through that horrific death and punishment for my sin, surely (with His help) I can keep my mouth shut and endure without sinning.

This is truly hard for me sometimes. I think this can go beyond bosses, and it can be a reminder for other relationships and encounters. For example, when our purchases or orders are wrong or late, we choose grace. When our husbands or coworkers say something out of crankiness, we choose not to fire something back at them.

3. "He himself bore our sins in his body so that we might die to sin." (verse 24) How are we to die to sin? Ask Jesus to show you your sin, grieve it, and ask Him for forgiveness and a heart to change and repent. It's easy for me to go about my days, forgetting to take time to examine myself and make an effort to continually die to sin. It can creep in and be hindering our relationship with Jesus and others, even if we don't realize it.

"By His wounds we are healed." (verse 24) This is spiritual healing. We will also be physically healed in heaven, but right now, we can begin to spiritually heal because of the blood that He shed. Thank you, Jesus.

Family Worship

Those two words (family worship) cause many parents to go, "Huh?" Let me explain. Family worship is a time when your family intentionally gathers and worships Jesus together. Worshipping with your church family is wonderful and necessary but worshipping with your little (or big) family at home is just as important. What happens at home sets a strong foundation for your children.

Family Worship is a precious time for our family. It isn't always peaceful and without training, but it is always worth it. Our kids miss it on nights when we are unable to make it happen.

Here's what it looks like in our home. After taking their baths and putting their pj's on, we gather in the living room on the couch. We begin with singing. Each child picks his or her favorite song about or to Jesus. These include but are not limited to:

"Jesus Loves Me"
"Jesus Loves the Little Children"
"Amazing Grace"
"Holy, Holy, Holy"
"I've Got Peace Like a River"
"It Is Well with My Soul"

It's amazing how our son memorized those hymns so quickly, even though he was only two years old.

My husband then prays, and that's it. We send them off to bed.

In the past, we read through a children's Bible, such as *The Jesus Storybook Bible* (our favorite). We may work that back in soon. Family Worship doesn't have to be elaborate or the ideal. Any time spent emphasizing our love for Jesus and worshipping with your children is precious in the sight of the Lord. Singing, reading, and praying before bed as a family really sets the tone for the end of the day. We long to glorify God and show our gratitude. In return, we receive His peace and joy as we drift off to sleep.

When speaking of his father, Missionary John Patton said,

When, on his knees and all of us kneeling around him in Family Worship, [our father] poured out his whole soul with tears … for every … need. We all felt as if in the presence of the living Savior and learned to know and love Him as our Divine Friend.

DAY 11

TODAY'S READING

1 Peter 3:1–6

1. How can we submit biblically to our husbands? This does not mean that we are not equal, that we are of less value, or that we have to do whatever they say. However, this does mean that God has set up an order. He says and shows us throughout scripture that a man is to be the head of the house. Men have different skills, gifts, and callings. We, as wives, have different skills, gifts, and callings. How can you support your husband in his calling? For those who are not married, how can you support men in their becoming leaders?

2. How can we teach our sons and daughters this biblical principle?

3. Respect and honor begin in the home. Our example is so powerful that unbelieving men can be won over to Christ. I know a woman who after fifty years of marriage to an unbeliever is finally seeing him attending church and reading scripture with her. The fruit of her faithfulness is coming to light after enduring all these years.

4. Read verses 3–4. Does this mean that we shouldn't get dressed up or braid our hair? No. It means that our beauty shouldn't come from those things. That type of beauty is fleeting. It fades. Real beauty comes from a gentle and quiet spirit. This convicts me. It is a whole lot easier to just wear more makeup and put my hair up than face my sin or areas of my heart that are in need of work.

Gracious Father,

Thank you for your love and grace to us. Thank you that you have gone before us this week and nothing surprises you. We trust you with our lives and families.

Lord God, you have called us to live set apart from the world. Please give us the grace, wisdom, humility, and strength to serve and submit in an honoring way to our husband's leadership. Help us not to nag or be unreasonable, to respect and value his opinions, and to encourage him in leading our family.

Please help us to show love and kindness. We ask forgiveness for the times that we haven't been kind, gentle, humble, and self-controlled. May your Spirit fill and lead us in a gentle and quiet way so that peace will reign in our homes and our children will want to follow our example. May our husbands, children, families, and friends see you in us.

We are world changers. We are raising up arrows for spiritual warfare. Please help us train, teach, serve, and love well. We have a high calling, but thankfully, it comes with your power and help. Thank you, Jesus. Amen.

Survival Tip #6

Memorize Scripture and Cling to It

When I was surrounded by toddlers, I began to understand how easy it could be to let my heart become hardened to their whining, pleas, and ultimately, their needs. It was constant. It was hard. My ears physically hurt. Sometimes they still do.

Then I was reminded of this verse, and I began to cling to it like my life depended on it.

And the King will answer them, "Truly, I say to you, as you did it to one of the least of these … you did it to me. (Matthew 25:40)

Every time, I quenched their thirst with another bottle or sippy cup, it was like quenching the thirst of my Savior. Every time I scooped them up from a fall, it was like comforting Jesus. Every time I made a meal, washed their clothes, kissed their faces, cleaned their hands, sympathized with their broken hearts, and got down on the floor to play, I was serving my King.

The least of these includes my children. The least of these includes your children. It is an honor and privilege to serve, love, cherish and sacrifice for them … for Him. That verse has carried me through many long, long days. What verse or verses can you memorize and cling to during this season?

DAY 12

TODAY'S READING

1 Peter 3:7

1. If you are not married, but you are hoping to be, please pray that your future husband, father, brother, or son will become the kind of man that is in this scripture. If you are married, please pray for all of the above and for our husbands, with me.

2. We do not read these verses to our husbands and instruct them in the way they should live. We also do not take offense at being the weaker vessel. To be honest, I like knowing that men are generally stronger emotionally and physically and that they can be very good protectors and pillars for us to lean on when we are stressed and worried. I don't mind it, but it is countercultural for me to say so. What are your feelings about it?

3. This verse ends with strong words regarding the consequence our husbands face if they do not treat us with respect.

Lord God,

Thank you for the men in our lives. Thank you for their protection, strength, wisdom, and courage. I pray, Father, they would be convicted over ways that they are not giving proper respect and love to us. I ask that you give them grace and forgive them. Please raise them up as courageous leaders, who are compassionate and strong. Make them men who fear and love you, seek to know you, and teach their children about you.

I pray they would make their relationships with you, their wives, their children, and their church a priority over worldly success and that they would flee any temptations of this world. Please help us to respect and honor them with our words and actions.

Thank you for the men in our lives. Thank you for the future men and women we are raising up. Please help us to train them well. Thank you, Jesus. Amen.

Snack Mix and Nonessentials

There are parenting essentials (commands) that are outlined in scripture and easy to acknowledge, such as discipline is good, loving kindness is expected, show compassion, teach your children the ways of the Lord, and feed, clothe, and care for one another. There's also a Christlike love of protecting them from spiritual, physical, mental, and emotional harm.

Then there are the nonessentials. Too often as mothers today, we get hung up on the nonessentials and neglect some of the essentials. If scripture isn't clear about something, we must seek the Spirit's leading through prayer and godly counsel. If it still isn't clear, you have freedom to do what you think is best and trust the Lord to aid you and your children. These nonessentials are often topics of unnecessary arguments between moms and dads, moms and other moms and moms and their own moms.

Sometimes I begin to fret and worry over a nonessential, and I have to stop myself and speak truth like this: "Kara, this is not in scripture. Pray on it and move freely about the premises." Here are some of the nonessentials I am referring to:

1. Should we send our kids to public school, private school, or homeschool them?
2. Should we feed our kids organic, packaged, traditional, gluten-free, homemade, or canned food?
3. Should we allow any screen time in our home?
4. Should we breastfeed or bottle-feed our babies?
5. Should I stay home with the kids or work outside of the home?
6. Should we have a big birthday party or a private family birthday party?
7. Should our kids participate in extracurricular activities at age five or should we wait until they are twelve?
8. How many activities are too many?

See what I mean? You may have felt your blood pressure rise on a couple of those. However, they really are nonessentials. Pray, trust, don't judge, encourage, and move on.

Oh, and speaking of how to best feed our kids, here is a nonorganic, traditional snack mix. However, you can make it to best suit your nonessential preferences.

Goldfish crackers+Cheerios+M&M's=yummy

I usually eat all of the Cheerios and M&M's out of the bowl. They are so good together.

DAY 13

TODAY'S READING

1 Peter 3:8–12

1. These four verses can be so challenging. When people are rude or criticize us or our children, it is so tempting to give them a little piece of our minds, isn't it? Or at the very least, we want to keep them at a distance, treat them with disdain, or tell twenty people how much they hurt us. Instead, we are being asked to be humble and to repay evil with blessing. We cannot do this alone. We can ask Jesus for help.

2. How do we bless them? We can pray for them, hope good for them, and if given the opportunity, show them love and compassion. This does not mean that you keep welcoming a toxic or abusive person into your life. You can be wise and distance yourself while at the same time praying for that person and not retaliating.

3. This passage is also a good reminder for inside our homes and not just outside. Are we sympathetic to our spouse and children? Are we loving, compassionate, and humble as we parent and serve?

Those are all great checks for our hearts. I'll leave us with the encouragement to spend time praying as you feel led today. Maybe you can ask God to show you the true state of your heart toward people (of all ages) in your life and ask for His help in loving others. You are an amazing woman who has been chosen by God for such a time as this.

Survival Tip #7

Choose Your Battles

Robin, my wise, beautiful sister is the mother of four amazing young adults. Robin shared these three wise words with me when I was about to get married, "Choose your battles." Those words have stuck with me through not only marriage but also parenting and church ministry. My sister is such a gift. She has had to either let go of or choose to fight many battles on behalf of children in the community as school principal, her own children as momma bear, and her marriage as a devoted wife. She and her husband love Jesus, give generously, and are creating a lasting legacy to the glory of God.

When she taught me that phrase, I had no idea how often I would use it. I've learned that if I nag my children over every little thing, never allow them to choose their favorite cup, do not empathize but only instruct, or try to focus on everything they need to learn all at once we quickly burn out in frustration. You have to decide which behavior to focus on for that season. Then you need to factor in how tired they are, how hungry they might be, and anything else that has been going on in their lives that week. Choose your battles. Sometimes they just need a hug and a do-over. Don't we all?

Sometimes even the messy sensory bin or play-dough experiment is worth the laughs, smiles, and peaceful moments of play. The same is true of marriage, as Robin shared with me fourteen years ago. Is the relationship worth the argument? Is forfeiting peace this evening worth the hill I'm fighting to die on? Sometimes, the answer is *yes*. Most of the time, I would argue that it is not. Take it to the Lord in prayer and enjoy the relationship. Life is short.

Do not provoke your children to anger but bring them up in the discipline and instruction of the Lord. (Ephesians 6:4)

A continual dripping on a rainy day and a quarrelsome wife are alike. (Proverbs 27:15)

DAY 14

TODAY'S READING

1 Peter 3:13–17

1. When we suffer for doing good, we will be blessed. When the scripture tells us to have no fear of them, who was the *them* that he was referring to? Peter originally wrote this to Christians who were confused and discouraged by the persecution they were facing because of their faith. The level of persecution they faced would send us shaking to our knees.

It's nothing like that today, at least not in our country. God gave us this letter in His Word because we do face persecution on a small level sometimes. It's very possible that we may face it on a larger level before we die. That's so encouraging, right? Thankfully, we have Peter's encouragement, which shows us how to endure.

2. I'm thankful for the blessing that Peter talked about here. He also reminded us to live above reproach so that slander and accusations wouldn't be true. My family and I pray often for the courage to lead our ministries with love, boldness, and faith. How about you? Do you face persecution from family, friends or coworkers because of your faith? What keeps you going?

> We cannot please all men, but we can be a blessing to many.
> —Mac Canoza

> Yet as persecution—even worldwide persecution—ensues against the Church there
> will be unity that will come, which will only be explainable as a miracle.
> —Principles Book

One man with truth on his side is stronger than a majority in error and will conquer in the end.
—Philip Schaff, 1882

To suffer and to be despised—what bitterness, but what glory.
—St. Therese of Lisieux

The nation doesn't simply need what we have. It needs what we are.
—St. Teresia Benedicta

Water Play Saves the Day

- Do you have a fussy kiddo? Throw him or her in the tub with lots of bubbles. This action has never failed me.
- Is your toddler bored? Run a little water into the sink and let them splash and wash their play dishes and toys.
- Is it summer? Take them to a pool, lake, or pond or fill up the baby pool. Chances are, everyone, including you, needs a day in the sun.
- Is it scorching hot? Sit on the porch with a glass of sweet tea in one hand and the other with your thumb firmly planted on the end of the water hose. Spray your kiddos like there is no tomorrow. There's nothing like a Midwest sprinkler.
- Are they filthy? Create a homemade car wash with a bucket of soapy water and a hose. Give your kids sponges and line up their outdoor ride-on toys, your car, your truck, or even the dog.
- Too much energy? Spray the trampoline or slide with water. It's the little things that count.
- Need more sensory play? Create a muddy puddle with the hose and make mud pies.
- Is it cleaning day? Fill a spray bottle with water and give the kids rags to wipe down counters, cabinets, toys, floors, and windows and water the flowers.
- Is it winter? Fill the bathtub with snow. Add toys from the movie *Frozen*, some paint brushes with watercolors, and some spoons. Our kids love it.
- Is it raining? Grab your umbrellas (or don't) and dance in a calm, warm rain. It will be the best day ever.

DAY 15

TODAY'S READING

1 Peter 3:18–22

1. Christ was crucified because of our sins and not His. It was the righteous for the unrighteous. Who are the unrighteous? We are. He died for us while we were still sinners. We didn't have to stop sinning and become perfect first. We were unrighteous when He died for us. If we repent and believe in that truth, we are made righteous. It's not that we don't sin anymore, but it's that God looks at us through the blood of Jesus, who makes us righteous (perfect, whole, and complete). Thank you, Jesus.

2. In verse 19, what did He proclaim, and who were the spirits? Many scholars believe that Jesus proclaimed the gospel to souls who had been in limbo for a long time. They died before Christ was crucified, so they hadn't heard the gospel. He gave them an opportunity.

3. Baptism in the Bible is talked about in a couple of different ways: spiritual and physical. When Jesus was baptized, He went under the water, and then He was brought back up. Baptism is linked to the resurrection of Christ. Baptism must be a spiritual event and not just a physical one. It represents the death of sin and resurrection of new life.

Other places in scripture tell us to repent and be baptized, which is why I personally believe you first have to be of an age to repent and believe the gospel before being baptized, but that's my interpretation. I do not believe the act of physical baptism saves you or promises you salvation, but I do believe that it is more important and spiritual than some believe it to be. My pastor-husband describes it as, "A physical participation in a spiritual reality." I love that. Have you been baptized? Why or why not? If so, what was your experience like?

4. I love to ask myself, *Why do I believe what I believe?* So why do you believe what you believe?

Lord Jesus,

Thank you again for your suffering, death, and resurrection. Thank you for the grace and faith to repent and believe. Please help us live today as new creations. Amen.

Survival Tip #8

Sunday Fun Day

As a pastor's family, we can easily become overwhelmed, drained, and exhausted on Sundays. For a season, I found myself dreading Sundays. They were often chaotic and unpredictable. However, when I am walking by His Spirit and with the greater good in mind, I can focus on turning this long day into a Sunday fun day for my family. It all starts with my preparation and attitude.

Six Tips for Sundays

1. Shoes

Jenny, a dear and super-organized friend and mother of six, shared this incredibly valuable tip. Keep your children's Sunday shoes together, on a closet shelf, and out of reach of little hands. Since implementing it, this tip has kept us from spending ten minutes looking for matching shoes every Sunday morning. I hope to learn more tips from Jenny soon. She has a house full of precious children, and she is one of the most peaceful women I know. She is also a gifted writer and knows just how to make me smile through her texts. I'm so grateful for her friendship.

2. To-Go Bags

When I'm on my game, I pack the busy bags, my Bible, and Sunday school teaching bag the night before. I put them by the door. Suckers and fruit snacks are a special treat during prayer time in our service. I also pack extra things for the restaurant that we go to after service.

3. Clothes

No matter how confident you are about what everyone is wearing on Sunday, lay it all out the night before so that you can double-check for wrinkles and stains. Remember to choose your battles. You can worship God in your Sunday best and also in your jeans and flip-flops. It is all about honoring

God, and we want to teach that to our children. If we panic and stress about looking perfect, we miss the mark before we even arrive at the building.

4. Children's Church

My husband and I see great value in sending our children downstairs for children's church. They sing with us and then head down just before the message. They learn so much down there. I am then able to listen and glean from solid biblical teaching without interruptions for thirty minutes. It's a win-win situation.

5. Sunday Sundaes or Pancake Night

Sometimes my husband and I make pancakes for the kids on Sunday nights. They really look forward to breakfast for dinner. It's an easy meal, and it helps us all unwind. Another idea is either going out for ice-cream sundaes or making them at home. It could become a fun weekly tradition. Do whatever it takes to help you relax, regroup, and reunite as a family.

6. Pray and Carry On

Ask for grace, extra patience, and peace in your home and the car ride to church. Ask for strength no matter what happens. Ask God to bless your time as a family and with your church family. He will provide for and lead you. Ask Him for ideas about ways to make it a day that honors Him, your husband, and your children.

DAY 16

TODAY'S READING

1 Peter 4:1–6

1. This scripture talks about suffering as Christ suffered. We don't often think of our suffering as something Christ also endured. Suffering can look like physical, emotional, or mental pain and hardship. It can be big or small in the world's eyes.

Verse 1 talks of suffering in the flesh as a way to kill sin. We can view suffering as a time to draw near to Christ. When we draw near to Christ, we are often able to defeat sin much easier. Drawing near to Christ may look like fasting from something, committing to daily time in prayer, reading His Word, or joining a church where His Word is taught, and people pray for and encourage each other.

What types of suffering have you endured or are currently experiencing? How are you handling it? How can you further lean into Christ during this difficult time?

2. Have you ever surprised someone by saying, "No," to going out and getting drunk, to gossiping, to drooling after a guy who wasn't your husband, or to engaging in any other un-Christlike behavior? Maybe others didn't understand, and you've lost or missed out on those friendships or fun times. It's so comforting to know that others may judge us according to the flesh, but God judges by the Spirit. Our reward is in heaven. Hang on. This world is tough and tempting, but you have a heavenly Father who is closer than your best friend, loves you unconditionally, and understands. Suffer well, sweet momma.

Thank you, Lord,

For showing us the purpose of and joy in suffering. Thank you for the grace and strength to say, "No," to ungodliness and to follow you. We love you. Amen

Parenting with Kindness

> There are three ways to ultimate success: The first way is to be kind. The second way is to be kind. The third way is to be kind.
> —Mr. Rogers

Our children treat others the way that they are treated. I make many parenting mistakes, and I will continue to do so, but I pray that my children will remember kindness, grace, and love shown to them by their mother. I encourage our children to always be kind—to each other and to themselves.

It has been proven that yelling is ineffective in disciplining children. (www.fatherly.com) The only time that I yell is if danger is a step away. Children respond best to calm voices. You can be stern, firm, instructive, administer consequences and still kind. You can be tired, hungry, frustrated, and overwhelmed and still be kind by the grace of God. It is so hard, but it is possible.

Kindness is disciplining in love and with patience. You know in your heart and spirit, if your tone, attitude, and expressions are not kind to your child. When this happens, and it does, I swallow my pride and apologize to my children. They see that I am human, but they also see that I ask for forgiveness, receive it, and move on with peace.

Renee, my Texas sister-in-law and the mother of two sweet kiddos, has one of the most tender hearts. She desires to parent well to the glory of God. All year long, we look forward to their summer visits to the farm. Renee shared these helpful tips for when the temptation to yell strikes:

- Take deep breaths and pray before you speak.
- Whisper when you want to yell.
- Remind yourself, *My kids are not for yelling at.*
- Don't forget to take time-outs to prevent burnout.
- When you mess up, ask for forgiveness.

    Love is patient and kind; love does not envy or boast; it is not arrogant or rude."
    (1 Corinthians 13:4)

Be kind and compassionate to one another, forgiving each other, just as in Christ God forgave you.
(Ephesians 4:32)

She opens her mouth with wisdom, and the teaching of kindness is on her tongue.
(Proverbs 31:26)

DAY 17

TODAY'S READING

1 Peter 4:7–11

1. Verse 7 says that the end of all things is at hand. People in every generation have believed that they could be the last ones or that Christ would come during their children's generation, so they said, "Be ready." That's a good thing. It's supposed to be like that because it keeps us busily sharing the gospel, repenting of sin, and looking for Jesus. Urgency makes us move.

2. In light of that mindset, we are to be self-controlled and sober-minded (think well and seriously about spiritual matters) "for the sake of our prayers." So it's not just our husband's prayers that are at stake.

3. Verse 8 tells us to keep loving one another earnestly, for love covers a multitude of sins. Love is full of grace, understanding, forgiveness, and compassion. How can we show more love today? Which person that God has placed in your path needs extra love today? Is it a child, a spouse, a fellow mom, a neighbor, or an elderly person at the grocery store?

4. Verse 9 says to show hospitality without grumbling. I believe this is becoming a lost art. Sometimes I really stink at it. Let's bring it back. Who can you invite for dinner or a playdate this week or month?

5. Verse 10 says that you are gifted. You have beautiful gifts that may need to be opened and used. Ask God what your gift is and how you can serve others with it. Look for ways that your gift has been affirmed and ask others what they think your gift is if you aren't sure.

My favorite part is the last part of verse 11: by the strength that God supplies. Hallelujah! We don't have to do it alone or in our own meager strength. God gives us His strength to love, serve, and live in godliness. Are you feeling weak? Just ask Him for His strength.

Survival Tip #9

Lean In

> Sometimes when you just feel like you need a break or you're going to explode, what you actually *need* to do is *lean in*. Tune your heart to your children. Do something small and quiet and cozy that they enjoy like read a book, bake a treat, or go for a walk. Sometimes the more alone time you get, the more you want. Sometimes the more you lean in, the easier it is to lean in.
> —Hannah, my kindred spirit and mom of four adorable young'uns

These words were texted to me from my sweet friend one night, and I couldn't agree with them more. Don't get me wrong. It's okay to take some mommy time and have some peace and quiet occasionally. You know your limit. Realistically though, we are in a season of dying to self, and without Christ, it would be easy to become bitter and develop a hardened heart while parenting. With the aid of His Spirit, we can indeed lean in and embrace this season. We can choose to smile, turn up the music or grab their favorite book, and tell our children how happy we are to be their mommas.

Make Memories and Cherish the Time

My beloved husband told me once, "You won't regret the time you spent just playing with them." He's so right. I never have, and I know that I never will. Ten years down the road, I will praise God for giving me the grace and strength to just sit and play, even when it tested my patience to the core and caused my to-do list to lengthen. They are worth it.

DAY 18

TODAY'S READING

1 Peter 4:12–19

1. Have you ever been surprised by a trial that you felt you didn't deserve? Or have you faced many trials at once and wondered why? I have often asked that question. Years ago, I was going to a female Christian counselor when she introduced me to these verses. It was the first time I realized that we get to share in Christ's sufferings when we face trials of many kinds. I began to see my trials as an honor. We get a tiny glimpse into what He did for us. Christ loves me so much that He refines and grows me in specific ways to bring Him more glory and to know Him more, which is all I want to do. The trials are not for our glory but His.

2. We get to experience a little of what Christ endured. Our suffering will never match His, but it does break His heart, and He does grieve with us. He loves us. As we learned in the beginning of 1 Peter, we suffer with the hope that Christ is coming. In this passage, Peter mentioned Christ's glory one day being revealed. I can't wait.

3. In verses 17 and 18, Peter also warned those who did not obey and believe the gospel. These warnings always prod me on to pray for those who are not saved, and I continue to share the gospel's message in every way that I know how. Think of one person who doesn't know Jesus who you can pray for.

Lord,

We love, praise, and thank you for the honor of sharing in your suffering. You were betrayed, mocked, and tempted. You lost loved ones and friends. You were ultimately crucified. Please give us strength for the various trials that we face today and in the near future. May our hearts remember these words right as we need them, and may they bring us much comfort. May we bring you glory.

We also lift up those who do not know you, are living disobedient lives, or have believed the lie that as long as they show up on Sundays, they are fine. Please save them. Please change their hearts and remove the veil from their eyes.

Thank you for being our faithful Creator. We entrust our lives and souls to you, as well as those of our children. We love you.

Teatime

If you are home with your children in the afternoons or on a lazy Saturday, teatime can be such a wonderful way to spend an hour. I'm a fan of nearly all things English. I have taken a fancy to the idea of stopping mid-afternoon for a cup of tea, a cookie, and pleasurable conversation. However, with toddlers, this looks more like apple juice in a teacup, Goldfish or animal crackers, and a lot of gentle reminders on etiquette and manners, which is honestly one of the many reasons I love teatime.

My soul sister Traci hosts the most wonderful tea parties with her daughter, complete with fancy teacups, flowers from their yard, a tablecloth, classic literature books, and an occasional guest flamingo. She has severe food allergies and still manages to provide such a creative and inspiring display for her little girl.

We call each other our "soul sister" because every conversation that we have centers on Jesus, discipleship, and how Biblical theology affects each area of our lives. I leave every conversation with her challenged, inspired, and closer to Jesus. We currently live 4.5 hours away from each other. I'm hoping our next conversation is over tea.

Reasons I Love Teatime with Children

- It's a perfect time to teach and review manners and table etiquette.
- It allows us all an opportunity to step away from screens and share a read-aloud book. We have read the Little House on the Prairie series, Dr. James Harriot's stories for children, and a few delightful and historical stories from American Girl.
- The children feel fancy, loved, cared for, and sought out. It is as if the queen herself is serving them tea. They giggle with glee.

- It's actually appropriate for both genders in England, so why not here? I often remind our son that he is a gentleman. He grins and finds that statement rather funny as an active three-year-old who makes as much noise as he can at all times.
- Some days, I select a children's devotional or character-building book. While they are sipping tea, it is a rare, quiet moment to lovingly address any character concerns.

How to Make It Extra-Special

- Find some eclectic teacups and saucers from a thrift store.
- Add milk first, then sugar, and top it with tea like the English do.
- Try various flavors of tea and let them vote on their favorite.
- Serve scones, biscuits, or little sandwiches to be proper.
- Invite their friends to join you.
- Dress up in costumes or fancy clothes.
- Bring their favorite stuffed animals or dolls to the party.

DAY 19

TODAY'S READING

1 Peter 5:1–5

1. At first glance, these verses may sound like they are only for pastors and don't apply to us, but, they do. First of all, they are qualities that you want to look for in your shepherd or pastor. Secondly, it tells us how to be good church members. We are to be humble and easy for our shepherd. We are to be humble toward one another and respectful of our pastors. Are you a churchgoer who is easy to shepherd? Do you respect your pastor? Is he a biblical leader?

2. God opposes the proud but gives grace to the humble. I think the mom arena can be a hard place to remain humble. It's so easy to compare ourselves with others and look for constant affirmation. Today's passage is a great reminder that God gives grace to the humble and that we all desperately need His grace and not His opposition. This is always a tough heart-check for me. Where does pride creep into your life? How does it affect your parenting, marriage, and job?

Father,

Please forgive us for comparing our skills, parenting, homes, and children to others. Please forgive us for judging, criticizing, and puffing ourselves up. We desperately need your grace. Please help us to live humbly and peaceably and encourage other moms and kids, celebrating with them and letting the nonessentials go. Anything essential to parenting is in your Word. Everything else is just a preference. We are all on this journey together.

Thank you for your love, mercy, strength, and hope. Please fill us with joy as we go about our day. We also lift up our pastors and elders and pray that they will have wisdom, humility, and grace. Please protect and bless their families. We want to be a joy for them to shepherd. If they are serving or teaching in ways that are not honoring to you, please convict and bring an end to it. May your name alone be glorified. Please grow our churches and help us to know and love you more. Amen.

Survival Tip #10

You Do You

> Comparison is the thief of joy.
> —Theodore (Teddy) Roosevelt

When I was very new to parenting, I doubted my every move. My precious sister-in-law, Becca, who is a terrific mother of three awesome kids, was so kind to serve as a listening ear. She has the gift of empathy and puts up with our crazy family with such grace. I'm so thankful for Becca. I remember that she kept saying, "It's okay. She'll outgrow it," "I don't think you have anything to worry about," or, "You are doing great. She seems fine to me." They were encouraging words of peace to my weary heart. There was no comparison or judging.

I had been comparing myself to other mothers and my baby to other babies, as if mine was really the only one in the universe not sleeping (or whatever the problem was that day). I still do this at times. It's amazing that when we compare, we only see the beautiful, good, happy, and better-than-us views. We seem to be suddenly blinded to the suffering, hurt, brokenness, or even sameness of many others around us. We are not unique in our challenges or less than, just because in a certain area, our neighbor seems to be more than.

You are called to be the mother of the children under your roof. You are unique to them, and they are unique to you. If God wanted another woman to be their mother, she would be, but she isn't. Keep your eyes fixed on the One who has called you, and He will give you all that you need.

Turn off social media if you need to. At least, unfollow people if you are tempted to fall into the trap of jealousy or comparison when you see their images. We all know that a Facebook post is only half the story anyway. Be the biggest fan of the other moms in your circle. The best words you can speak to a fellow momma of littles are, "You are doing amazing." Yes, you are, sweet momma. Yes, you are.

DAY 20

TODAY'S READING

1 Peter 5:6–8

1. There it is again: humbling ourselves. It is so tough. But when we exult ourselves, it doesn't leave us with any true fulfillment. When I exalt myself, I fall flat on my face. Have you taken a minute to repent of any pride? Your Shepherd is waiting with His loving arms open wide.

2. Verse 6 goes on to explain that if we humble, submit, and surrender to the mighty hand of God, He will exalt us when the time is right. That type of exultation brings glory to God, and it is part of His purpose and plan for us. It's lasting and freeing. What can you submit to God and surrender control over?

3. Verse 7 is a challenging one for me. My list of anxieties is long—really long. But we are to cast or throw those anxieties onto Him. Why? Because He cares for us. The Creator of the universe cares for you, right now, with your messy bun, grumpiness, weariness, and stress or your hair straightened, makeup on, yet still tired and feeling less than perfect you. Hallelujah! What a Savior, Friend, and wonderful Father we have. Now that's true strength and hope for whatever this week may hold. Say this with me, "God cares for me."

Thank you, Jesus,

Thank you for caring for us when it sometimes feels like no one else does. You see our tears, suffering, sacrifices, and our sin. You know our fears. You love us anyway. Please forgive us of the pride that creeps in and help us to keep our eyes on you. We don't want to compare or exult ourselves. We want to bring glory and to honor to you and love and fear you above all else. Please help us to do just that, Father. Thank you. Amen.

Letting Go of Control

Our firstborn was only twelve months old, and I had hit my breaking point. We were driving in the car late one night on our way home from church ministry when I unleashed myself on my beloved husband. In my mind, he could be helping me a thousand times more. In my mind, he wasn't doing anything at all (not true). I was tired.

My patient, loving husband was silent for a moment. Then he calmly turned and spoke these life-changing words: "I love you, and I appreciate all you do for our daughter. I would love to help you more. I've wanted to help you more. I've tried to help you more. You haven't let me."

What? I thought. Before I had a chance to fire back, the Holy Spirit convicted me right then and there. He was right. I had told him early on not to get up in the night because I needed to feed her, and he would just prolong the inevitable. I had prevented him from giving her baths or dressing her because I had a certain way of doing it. I criticized him if he didn't do things the way that I would do them. I did it all in the name of I'm the mother, and I know best. My family can all testify that I have control issues when it comes to our children. God has been working with me on them for a long while now. It involves regular repentance and daily grace.

Two kids later, and I couldn't be happier when Ryan jumps in and takes over. I've learned to let go of control (mostly) and accept his methods. Now, I am so thankful that I can rely on him for an answer to their problems. When a child screams and he is home, I walk the other way. It turns out that our children need both of our methods. I know that I'm slow to realize these truths. God gave them a mom *and* dad and He has specific purposes for each one. They need his tickles after a long day with mom, and they also need his authority when momma is tired of correcting. They need his affection and Superman powers while I administer the meds. We are a team—Team Edwards.

But He said to me, "My grace is sufficient for you, for my power is made perfect in weakness." Therefore, I will boast all the more gladly of my weaknesses, so that the power of Christ may rest upon me. (2 Corinthians 12:9)

DAY 21

We are wrapping up 1 Peter today. Can you believe it? In this crazy season of life, you have studied an entire book of the Bible. Praise, Jesus!

TODAY'S READING

1 Peter 5:8–14

1. Verse 8 is such a good reminder to not get caught up in the distractions of this world because we do have an enemy, and we need to be alert. He wants to kill God's people spiritually and physically. We know who has the final say and victory, so we don't have to live in fear, but we do need to be wise. Satan wants you to believe his lies about you and about others. Be alert. Tell him, "No!" aloud and turn on the praise and worship music.

2. Verse 9 points out that you are not alone. Your brothers and sisters in Christ are in the same battle. What fire have you recently walked through? How does it help when someone who has been there and done that reaches out to you? Who can you reach out to today and encourage in that same way?

3. Verse 10 is about hope. After we have suffered a little while, God, who is so gracious, will personally restore, confirm, strengthen, and establish us. Praise God! To Him be all glory. Hold on, dear sisters. Help is on the way.

4. In verse 12, I love how he ends with one more exhortation: Stand firm in the true grace of God. Grace is undeserved but given because of Jesus's sacrifice. Stand firm. You are His if you have received the gifts of repentance and faith.

5. Verse 14 tells us to greet one another kindly and with love (Sorry, I won't be kissing you, but I'm for sure a hugger) and to receive Christ's peace. Do you greet one another with love and kindness at home? Is Christ's peace welcome in your home? Shalom.

Keto-Friendly and Gluten-Free Chicken Fingers

Ingredients

- 2 cups almond flour
- 2 tablespoons paprika seasoning
- 2 teaspoons salt and pepper
- 2 eggs
- 2 cups buttermilk
- 8 chicken breasts cut into thick strips
- 1 stick of butter

Preparation

1. Mix the flour, paprika, salt, and pepper and set on a plate.
2. In a large bowl, mix eggs and buttermilk. Then begin soaking chicken strips in the milk-and-egg mixture (as many as will fit at a time).
3. Melt butter in pan on the stove on medium-high heat.
4. Using tongs, pull out a chicken strip from the milk-and-egg mixture and rub it in the dry flour mixture on the plate.
5. Drop the coated strip in the pan of melted butter.
6. Repeat until the bottom of the pan is filled with one layer of chicken.
7. Cover with a lid and watch them fry. After five minutes or so, turn the strips over to fry the other sides.
8. Strips are finished when the center is white and juices run clear and hot.

Serve with ketchup, a salad, and/or mashed potatoes. You can use the leftover skillet mess to make gravy or keep it simple with chips and fruit or make your own chicken sandwich. Let the kids make tunnels and slides out of the pillows in the living room after lunch, and you'll feel like you are at Chick-Fil-A (almost).

DAY 22

TODAY'S READING

2 Peter 1:1–4

Welcome to the second letter of Simon Peter. He wrote this to the believers, so if you are a Christ follower, you will glean much wisdom and truth from this letter.

1. How do we obtain precious faith? (see verse 1) We obtain it by the righteousness of our God and Savior, Jesus Christ. It isn't by our works or good behavior, but it is through His righteousness that we are saved. We will never be good enough.

2. We learn in verse 2 that God has given us all things that pertain to life and godliness. What are those things exactly? Jesus's sacrifice on the cross, His resurrection, the Holy Spirit to minister to us, faith, forgiveness of sins, love, prayer, angels, the Bible, biblical teachers, our church family, and brothers and sisters in Christ.

3. They came with exceedingly great and precious promises (see verse 4). I love that. Why did He give them to us? He gave them so that we might be partakers of the Spirit of God—His divine nature. We are image bearers. Christ is in us.

4. What did we escape through His merciful act of salvation? The end of verse 4 says that we escaped the corruption that is in the world of lust. This lust isn't only sexual but an unhealthy hunger and an uncontrolled and unsatisfying desire for idols and the emptiness of this world. Are there any areas of your life where you are still lusting and longing after something in this world—something that will not bring you lasting hope and peace like the gifts from God do?

Father,

You are a good, good Father, who knows how to give exceedingly great and precious promises and gifts to your children. Thank you for Jesus's sacrifice on the cross and resurrection. Thank you for the Holy Spirit who was sent to empower and minister to us, for faith, forgiveness of sin, love, prayer, angels to also minister to us, the Bible, biblical teachers, our church family, and our brothers and sisters in Christ, near and far. Thank you for delivering us from the darkness of this world and filling us with your light and goodness.

May we bring glory and honor to your name. Please cleanse us from any remaining impurity and continue to form us into your likeness. As we continue our study of Peter's letters, please open our eyes, hearts, and minds to your truth. May we apply it to our lives by your grace and mercy. Amen.

A Week in the Life

Here is an excerpt from an article I posted on TodaysChristianFamily.com.[1]

This has been a "hubby suffered a heat stroke, cat got run over, milk spilt under the fridge" kind of week, and it's only Wednesday … There have been many other personal issues come up the past few days, but I won't bore you with those. It is during *these* weeks though I have to stop and say, "Okay, Lord. You have my attention." This frustrating and hard season seems to never end. The Lord reminded me today there is something else that is truly never-ending.

But my people have changed their glory for that which does not profit. Be appalled, O heavens, at this; be shocked, be utterly desolate, declares the LORD, for my people have committed two evils: they have forsaken me, the fountain of living waters, and hewed out cisterns for themselves, broken cisterns that can hold no water. (Jeremiah 2:11–13)

Do you ever feel like a broken cistern that cannot hold any water? You keep trying to fill yourself up, but you continually feel drained? God refers to Himself as "the fountain of living waters." He is never-ending.

When we have forsaken Him and turned to our own glory, we are broken. When we look for satisfaction in this world and the things of this world, we find it isn't lasting. When we try to use our good deeds or our abilities to strive forward on our own, we come out dry and empty. Only through His comforting, healing, and redeeming work on our hearts can we experience the grace, strength, and satisfaction that we need and deeply desire. He is an unending mountain spring. We best glorify and enjoy Him when we are on our knees drinking continually, having our strength renewed and thirst quenched.

So this week, we are on our knees and drinking from the springs of living water. Jesus alone satisfies. I need Thee every hour.

DAY 23

TODAY'S READING

2 Peter 1:5–9

1. What is "this very reason"? Looking back at the previous two verses, the reason is that we have been given all things that pertain to godliness. We are rescued from corruption by the grace of God. It's beautiful to watch these attributes (see verse 5–7) unfold, grow, and manifest themselves in a believer's life.

2. These are the fruits of having the Spirit in us as believers. If we don't have fruits, we need to examine our hearts. Verse 8 says that if these things (mentioned above) are yours and they abound (or are increasing, as the English Standard Version says), we will have the knowledge of Christ and confirm our election to the family of God. Do they abound in your life? We are still sinners being made new, but what is the pattern of your life? Are you growing in these areas?

3. If they are not evident in our lives, it says that we have forgotten that we were cleansed (see verse 9) or haven't experienced salvation in the first place. Your Father is a good Father. Do you remember the good gifts that He gives? His arms are open. His forgiveness is ready, and His love is immeasurable. Run to Him, sweet sister. Cry out. He is kind and merciful.

Thank you, Jesus,

For salvation and leading us on the path of righteousness. Your path leads to love and not to selfish ambition. When we climb the ladder of faith, we end up looking more like you. When we focus on climbing the ladder of this world, we are left broken and empty. Please give us grace and fill us with your

Spirit so that we can have life abundantly in you. Convict us of any ungodliness in our lives and help us to leave it at your feet. We love you and long for our families and ourselves to worship you alone. May our fruits abound today as we love, care for, teach, guide, and serve our children. In Jesus's name, amen.

Praying Over Your Spouse

I do not cease to give thanks for you, remembering you in my prayers. (Ephesians 1:16)

How often do you pause and pray for your spouse? Too often, I worry about Ryan, get frustrated with him, and even forget about his needs, before I remember to stop and pray for him. Prayer is our best offense and defense in marriage. As believers, it is the greatest that tool we have been given for the marital relationship. God is for marriage. He is eager to hear you cry out on behalf of your spouse, and He is ready to act on your behalf and his for His glory and your good.

I cannot tell you how many times in our fourteen years of marriage that I have been burdened with frustration toward my husband, a miscommunication, or hurt that I didn't know how to convey. When I turned to the Lord in prayer instead of confronting him immediately, I saw God work powerfully in both of our hearts. It's not that I pray, and God brings my husband crawling to my feet apologetically. I can't just get what *I* want or what *I* think is best. It's not about me. It's that God proves over and over that He is for *us* and marriage. He softens both of our hearts. He draws us to Himself and to each other.

Here are some specific ways to pray for your husband.

Lord,

I thank you for _____. We don't always agree, and we have changed a lot over the years. I pray that you would unite us in love. Please increase our affections toward one another. May _____ be attracted to me physically and emotionally. Help me to love him the way that you do and see him with your eyes.

Faith

Pray for an increase of faith and knowledge of the Lord and a longing for the Lord and the things of the Lord. Pray that he would love the Lord will all his heart, soul, mind, and strength and hate evil.

Protection

Pray for physical (safety), spiritual (biblical teaching and reading), emotional (offenses and discouragement), and mental (controlling thoughts and believing truth) protection.

Repentance

Pray that any sins would be revealed to him, that he would confess them to Jesus, and that Jesus would forgive and grant him repentance.

Wise

Pray that he would be wise in parenting, in leading in the home, and with finances and that he would use his talents and resources wisely. Pray that he would be wise in any decisions that may arise that day.

Health

Pray that God would bless his health and cause him to have healthy habits.

Friendships

Pray that he would have strong friendships with other people who love Jesus and will encourage his faith and family commitments.

Work

Pray that the work of his hands would be blessed, he would find favor with his employers, and he would be fruitful in all that he does.

Marriage

Pray for faithfulness and purity in your marriage. Pray that you both would have thoughts, actions, and desires to grow in intimacy with one another. May truthfulness, kindness, and grace set the tone of the home and your marriage.

Ministry

Pray that God will bring opportunities to serve, help others, and use your marriage to point others to Jesus.

What a gift to be able to take our concerns, fears, and frustrations to Jesus, who can actually do something about them. As you begin to pray more and more for your husband, I believe that you will see God work in amazing and mysterious ways in both of your hearts and lives. May your marriage be full of His goodness and Christ be glorified.

DAY 24

TODAY'S READING

2 Peter 1:12–15

1. Why did Peter keep reminding us of these qualities? Do you grow weary of the measuring stick? Even though we know about them and may even be established in these truths, he reminded us because it was what people needed to hear and we do too. Peter was about to die, and the words that we are studying are the ones that he chose to write in his last letter. This letter really needs to count, and this is what the Holy Spirit inspired him to write. That's how important these words are. Let's lean in and pay attention to each word, even if we have been told these truths a million times before.

2. Do you see these characteristics growing in your children? If so, write them a letter today encouraging them and pointing out the ways that they look more like Jesus. If not, don't be too disheartened. Your God is mighty to save, and He loves your kids more than you do. Ask God for help to know how to encourage and teach them. Ask Him to give them hearts that will receive the truth and be saved. You could also write them a letter and share your own testimony or story of your relationship with Christ and the ways in which you are growing and being challenged. They might be very encouraged by your own authenticity and honesty.

Lord Jesus,

Thank you for your Word. Thank you that this is one of the main ways we hear you speaking to us. Please help us to listen. We pray that our children will have a strong desire for your Word and will hunger for it, grow in it, and receive it in faith. We pray that we will never grow weary of the truth. Please open our eyes and ears to all things that are from you. May your strength and joy be found in our weakness today. Thank you, Jesus. Amen.

Survival Tip #11

Ninety-Nine Cent Spray Bottles

They are seriously ninety-nine cents apiece, come in a variety of colors, and offer your kids *hours* of entertainment. Kids love to control a spray bottle. What can they do with them that long? Allow me to share a tried-and-true list of options.

1. Clean the windows inside and out.
2. Water the plants inside and out.
3. Clean the shower or bathtub.
4. Combine it with a towel, and they can clean cabinet doors.
5. Spray each other outside on a hot day.
6. Clean their toys inside and outside.
7. Add another towel, and they can clean the floor as well as the baseboards, the walls, and the furniture.

It's okay if you make a mess, as long as you clean it up.
—Says me, only about a thousand times a day

DAY 25

TODAY'S READING

2 Peter 1:16–18

Woah! What? Peter was there? Let's back up a minute. I'm not a big fan of gathering all of the history and facts about a book before I dive into it. I like to go headfirst and then find answers to my questions as I go along. When my curiosity is peaked, I am better able to remember what I discover. Now that we are well on our way into his second and last letter, is your curiosity peaked? Let's answer some key questions.

1. Who was Peter? He was a leader among the twelve disciples of Jesus. Yes, he was often chosen to walk, talk, and eat with Jesus. He was also the same Peter whose name originally was Simon, and Jesus changed his name to mean spiritual rock. Out of fear, he ended up denying that he knew Jesus three times when the Romans arrested Jesus and threatened his followers. Can you blame him? Later, they also crucified Peter. Peter asked them to crucify him upside down because he wasn't "worthy to be crucified in the same manner as his Lord." (Stated in the apocryphal book, the *Acts of Peter.)* I'd say he was all in, fully committed, and a humbling example of the rock that the church was built on (see Matthew 16:13–19).

2. Verse 16 says that Peter was an eyewitness at Jesus's baptism when God the Father said, "This is My Beloved Son, with whom I am well pleased" (Matthew 3:17). He has credibility. Can you imagine being there and hearing that voice boom from the mountains? It gives me the chills to think about it.

3. Jesus chose to become fully man when he came to earth. To receive glory and honor from God was the best gift He could have been given. God the Father was pleased with His Son, and He made it publicly known. Jesus knew that His Father loved, cared for, supported, and approved of Him. This is also important in every parent-child relationship. How do you speak of your children publicly (Facebook)? When they hear you talking with other moms? How are you seeking to feel loved and appreciated? Have you rested in the truth of God your Father's love and acceptance of you?

Redefining Good

Recently our son developed a limp. We took him to the doctor and had X-rays taken, but we received no answers or real solutions. The doctor assured us that it was probably just a muscle strain or swollen joint and sent us on our way. Sure enough, she was right. But while I watched my usually active toddler painfully struggle just to walk, I grew impatient for his healing, and fear crept in. I thought, *What if this lasts a long time? What if we are missing something like a more serious condition? What if he compensates for the limp and causes damage to something else?*

I eventually said to myself, *Okay, you can play the what-if game, such as what if he walks with a limp for the rest of his life? Honestly, I would rather that he walk with a painful limp for the rest of his life and know and love Jesus than be a superstar athlete who is perfectly healthy and has full access to this world's pleasures.*

Did you catch that? I would rather my son have a personal relationship with Jesus Christ and not walk normally than win the Super Bowl, World Series, or even enjoy high school athletics. Can you honestly say that? If God chose to use a limp to teach my child to rely on and to trust in Him, so be it, and thank you, God, for being so gracious. My greatest prayer, above even physical safety, is for the salvation of our children. This is a tough one sometimes when I think of the extreme dangers in our world. Many evils much worse than death could happen to our children. They give me nightmares. I do pray for their safety and healing when they are hurt or sick, but more than anything, I pray for their salvation.

For those who live according to the flesh set their minds on the things of the flesh, but those who live according to the Spirit set their minds on the things of the Spirit. (Romans 8:5)

We have to shift our minds from the things of the flesh (ourselves and our physical world) to the things of the Spirit (the things of God, which are salvation, holiness, grace, and the fruits of the spirit). The things of God have true benefits, lasting pleasures, and eternal significance. Life is but a vapor.

My husband was having lunch with some men recently, and the topic of financial prosperity came up. Someone had taken a very expensive trip, lives in a mansion, and drives a dream car. It was mentioned that he and his wife are living the "good life." According to the world, it would appear so. He knows the person who is being discussed isn't a Christian. He's a good guy—kind, fun, and faithful to his spouse—but he doesn't have a personal relationship with Jesus and neither does his family. They do not have true hope. If that's the good life, please count me out.

Money can remove stress and help us enjoy luxuries in many ways. It is a blessing to those in need and can serve a good purpose. When we die though, our money is just handed to the next person. It doesn't go with us. Our souls, however, will either burn in hell and be forever separated from God or will be with God and living full perfect lives eternally at true peace. I wouldn't trade that for anything. A shopping spree or mocha frap bring me momentary comfort, but true peace, lasting joy, and hope that gets me through the daily grind, the greatest disappointments, and the hardest moments is only found in Jesus. I can't imagine living this life without Him.

For we do not have a high priest who is unable to sympathize with our weaknesses, but one who in every respect has been tempted as we are, yet without sin. (Hebrews 4:15)

Because, if you confess with your mouth that Jesus is Lord and believe in your heart that God raised him from the dead, you will be saved. (Romans 10:9)

But he was pierced for our transgressions; he was crushed for our iniquities; upon him was the chastisement that brought us peace, and with his wounds we are healed. Isaiah 53:5

And my God will supply every need of yours according to his riches in glory in Christ Jesus. Philippians 4:19

Now someone please remind me of this truth the next time my child is sick or in pain.

DAY 26

TODAY'S READING

2 Peter 1:19–21

1. Peter's heart and passion in his last letter are there to help us believe that the accounts really did happen and the prophecies from years ago have come true.

2. How much should we care about the prophecies about Jesus coming true? Imagine being lost in the dark. It's pitch black. You don't know which sound is real or what is in front of your face. Then a light shines out of nowhere, and your only hope is to cling to the path that is lit by that light until the sun comes up. That's what the confirmation of prophecies mean to us. They are the foundation of our faith. They are the steady light leading to the path.

The prophecy came from the Holy Spirit through the prophets who spoke them and wrote them down. We know that it was a true word because it came to pass. There are many prophecies about Jesus in the Old Testament. The Old Testament sets a beautiful foundation for the Messiah.

Jesus, our Savior,

You came, fully man, to live a perfect, blameless life. You taught us, left us the gifts of your Word and Spirit and then poured your blood out for us. You were blameless, yet you died for me and for every woman who is reading this book and praying this prayer with me. Jesus, please forgive us. We take your life and death for granted. We live in fear, worry, and doubt, and we wear selfish blinders. Please give us faith to see the lamp that is burning in front of us and giving us light until you return or call us home. By your grace and strength, may we pass these truths down to the next generation, and they pass them to the next generation, just as they were shared with us. Help us to devote our lives to the understanding, teaching, and savoring of your Word. You are our life, breath, and hope. Thank you, Jesus.

Isaiah 53:4-6 says,

Surely he has borne our griefs and carried our sorrows; yet we esteemed him stricken, smitten by God, and afflicted. But he was pierced for our transgressions; he was crushed for our iniquities; upon him was the chastisement that brought us peace, and with his wounds we are healed. All we like sheep have gone astray; we have turned—every one—to his own way; and the Lord has laid on him the iniquity of us all.

(Part of a prophecy concerning Jesus our Savior)

The Perfect Roast in the Crockpot

We raise beef—grass-fed, grain-finished, and mouthwatering Angus beef. Growing up as a farm girl was an absolute blessing, which I appreciated as a kid and appreciate even more now as an adult. I loved the wide-open spaces where I could let my imagination run wild. I loved the animals, the chores, the agricultural education I received, and the unique ways I could entertain friends. We rode four-wheelers, jumped bales of hay, fished, climbed seed bags, road in the tractor, and spent all night on the trampoline counting the bright shining stars.

Sure we were twenty-plus miles away from a movie theatre, bowling alley, in-crowd parties, and some other happenings (although I can't think of them right now). I wouldn't trade my upbringing, experiences, or the lessons I learned on the farm for anything.

In addition to the beauty of hard work, here are a few of those lessons.

- Don't try to lift a five-gallon bucket full of grain above your head and over the fence to feed the calves right before leaving for church service. Your head, pretty dress, tights, and shoes will be covered in grain.
- Turn the water hose off after filling the trough and before heading in for the night or you will have a new pond in the morning. Sorry, Dad.
- Close the gate or the sheep will get out.
- Don't follow your collie into the pen with a territorial ram unless you want to spend an hour with your pants caught on the barbed-wire fence.
- When backing out the four-wheeler, make sure that a parked combine isn't behind you.

- Close the gate or the cattle will get out.
- Highway patrolmen like to pull over speeding red cars, even on country roads.
- If you have to walk to the barn at night to do your chores and hear the coyotes howling, sing "Amazing Grace" there and back 101 times; it is very comforting.
- Watching my mom handle many farm emergencies and injuries with a level head prepared me for any trauma—except my own children's.
- Last but certainly not least, close the gate.

I'll stop reminiscing. Here's the recipe you've been waiting for.

Ingredients

- large enough roast to feed your family
- a crockpot
- 1 stick of salted butter
- pepper to taste
- onion flakes to taste
- carrots
- potatoes
- 1 cup water

Preparation

1. Place roast in crockpot.
2. Add the entire stick of butter.
3. Sprinkle with pepper and onion flakes.
4. Add carrots and potatoes (as many as you'd like or will fit).
5. Pour in water.
6. Turn crockpot on high and let it cook 8–10 hours.

When ready, serve with anything you like. It will be amazing. My mom says you can substitute turnips for potatoes so that it is keto friendly.

DAY 27

TODAY'S READING

2 Peter 2:1–3

We are about to delve into a heavy area and sensitive topic. I told my husband that I didn't think this letter of Peter's had ever been in a mommy devotional before, but I truly believe it is important. Even in this season of life, you can have good theology.

1. What comes to mind when you think of a false teacher or prophet? Have you ever known a pastor who was only after personal gain and used poor doctrine to draw a crowd? I have, which is why I boldly said that I would never marry a preacher. (Thankfully, God had other plans.)

2. What did Peter mean when he said that the Master *bought* them? He meant Jesus, the Master, paid the price of His life for them on the cross. They denied Christ by introducing secret lies, deceitful teaching and trying to pervert the truth.

3. Verse 3 assures us that God will deal with them and their souls. It is our job to be on alert. This is one of the many reasons I am passionate about women knowing their Bibles, having the confidence to use them, seeking to understand, and studying them for themselves. If you are around a teacher, pastor, or priest who does not encourage you to read and study your Bible, it should be a red flag.

Humans make mistakes. Even ones with good intentions can misspeak or misunderstand. Check everything you hear. Pray about it and ask the Holy Spirit to give you discernment and wisdom, even the things that I am sharing with you in this book. As we continue to be warned by Peter about false teachers, I'll be sharing in the coming days some specific warnings to look out for and ways to guard yourself and your family.

Survival Tip #12

The Dreaded "Achoo!"

Certain times of year—spring, summer, fall, and winter—seem to bring on nasty colds in our household. Watching your child struggle to breathe well enough to sleep and eat is so sad. You pray for it to pass quickly, but your heart sinks when you hear that deep-chest cough in the night. I hate colds. Over the past seven years, I have learned a few tricks to treat the symptoms and shorten the lifespan—*usually*. When it's time to enter sick mode, you can do the following things.

1. Disengage

We cancel everything and stay home for at least a few days. This gives the kids time to rest, eat, and drink as needed, and it keeps us from sharing our germs. Let's be honest, no one wants to see my snotty kids, and my kids honestly are not up for a lot of activity. They need long naps and lots of love.

2. Eucalyptus

Vaporizers and diffusers are turned on in bedrooms and the living room where they play and watch cartoons. I'm not the hippest mom when it comes to oils, but I do love to use eucalyptus and lavender.

3. A.M. Bath

Mornings and night are the worst for us regarding congestion and coughing. When it's bad, we start out the day with a warm bath to loosen the gunk. If throats are sore, I let them enjoy Popsicles during bath time. The treat gives them extra fluids and adds some smiles to those precious faces.

4. P.M. Bath

In the evening, we give the kids another warm bath with kid-friendly vapor bath soap. After their baths, Vicks BabyRub is great to rub on their feet and then cover their feet with cozy socks (My sister taught me that trick).

5. Get Dressed

We all feel better if we are dressed, makeup and all. After all, you never know who might stop by with a cup of soup or if you might need to run to the doctor's office.

6. Relax

This is not the time to fret or feel the mommy guilt of screen time. Whatever allows their bodies and you to rest (because you probably aren't getting much sleep either) is a good thing. Read books, snuggle, and put on some fun cartoons.

7. Fluids

Push the fluids: water in the bottle, warm water with honey, apple juice and water for the toddler, chicken broth in cups, and warm soup for supper with lots of herbs.

8. Drive

There have been times when we have not been able to get our babies to sleep because every time we laid them down, the gunk settled, and they coughed or couldn't breathe well. On those days, I loaded them in the car and just drove. It was relaxing for me because I didn't have to juggle, and they were upright in their car seats, so they could rest easier. It was a win-win situation.

I do have a disclaimer. I am in no way a health professional. My personal experience with essential oils and other tricks while fighting colds does not count as medical advice. We do additionally use children's cold medicines and pain relievers as needed.

DAY 28

TODAY'S READING

2 Peter 2:4–10

1. Peter was referring to the historical accounts of Satan and the angels' fall (see Revelation 12:9), the sparing of Noah during the flood (see Genesis 7), and the sparing of Lot from the destruction of Sodom and Gomorrah (see Genesis 19). Here we are reminded of God's justice, judgment, and discipline. However, we are also reminded of His salvation and deliverance.

2. After the stories of gloom, hope is found in verse 9: "The Lord knows how to rescue the godly from trials." Thank you, Lord. Our God is mighty to save. Are you in a trial? Did you need to hear this hopeful word today? The rescue may not be as swift or dramatic as we'd like, but be encouraged that you are not forgotten, you are not alone, and your God is able. Lean in, keep the faith, and cling to His Word.

3. Let's go back to the solemn reminder as we end this section. He is able to punish the ungodly. God punishes those who are against Him. If you are not for Him, you are against Him. Have you surrendered to Him? Are there any sinful habits that are keeping you from a right relationship with Christ? Confess it to Him today, ask for help, and surrender to His will for your life. He is quick to forgive and help His children. He is a good God.

4. Lastly, let's use the first part of verse 10 as fuel in our parenting today. As we instruct and train our children, we want to go to the heart of the matter. Do their hearts honor and respect authority? Do they have hearts that want to obey? Are we teaching them to have self-control? It is about more

than just outward behavior. As parent, we want to speak to their hearts and show them that their hearts need Jesus.

Lord God,

You are Mighty. You are Holy. There can be no sin, evil, or wickedness in your midst. I wouldn't want my God to be any less holy or powerful. Thank you for being our rescuer. Please deliver us from any sin that is keeping us from you.

As we parent, please help us train up our children in a way that speaks to their hearts. Please give them hearts to love you and their families, to obey and honor authority and have self-control, even in this ungodly world. We pray for wisdom in parenting and for purity in our own lives as we strive to live for you by your grace and strength. Thank you, Lord. Amen.

Homemade Bath Bombs

Call it what you wish: bath bomb or bath frizzle. All I know is that when we made these together, it was explosive but so much fun. It is a great sensory activity that works. The water turns a pretty blue or purple color, their skin is super soft afterward, and it opens their little sinus passages. Our daughters love bath bombs and always ask to purchase them when we are shopping at certain stores.

Now we can make our own and save money while enjoying a great indoor activity together. It also cleans up easily because of the simple ingredients. Your table will smell good and look clean with just a swipe of a wet washcloth.

Ingredients

- 1/2 cup cornstarch
- 1/2 cup Epsom salts
- 1 cup baking soda
- 2 1/2 tablespoons coconut oil
- water to sprinkle or spray on
- 10–12 drops of essential oil (eucalyptus, lavender, or whatever you like)
- food coloring
- mini-muffin tin

Preparation

1. Mix cornstarch, salts, and soda.
2. Add coconut oil, essential oil, and food coloring.
3. Combine well.
4. Begin spritzing with a little water at a time until you have a good consistency for packing the mix together. You want it to stick together, but if you add too much water, it will activate the bath bombs.
5. Pack into muffin tins.
6. Let sit for 24 hours.
7. Flip pan upside down and pop the bath bombs out.
8. Place in decorative treat bags, seal, and give away or set out in your bathroom ready for use. They look pretty in a bowl on your bathroom counter.

Add a bath bomb to your child's bathwater and enjoy the wonderful aroma and sparkling eyes of your child.

It's rare, but some children have had allergic reactions to Epsom salts. You may want to test a little mixed with water on their arms first.

DAY 29

TODAY'S READING

2 Peter 2:10–15

1. Verse 10 is very difficult to read but I learned so much while studying it. Originally, I thought it was referring to the saints. However, I learned that the literal term here is *glories*. It could refer to the glories we read about in 1 Peter 1:11, which was the Second Coming and exaltation of Christ. The false prophets of Peter's day (and our day as well) were so arrogant they denied and mocked the Second Coming of Christ and His glories. He goes on to say that the angels, who were more powerful, were not even *that* arrogant. This was confirmed again later in 2 Peter 3. No matter what Peter was referring to, the point is the false prophets were very, very arrogant and wrong.

2. Have you ever been around an irrational animal? On the farm, we have seen our fair share. These animals become wild eyed, and there is no working with them. We remove them from our farm as quickly as possible because they are dangerous. The same is true for false prophets, teachers, and leaders. They need to be removed quickly because they are dangerous. They poison the minds of young believers or those who are not solid in their faith. They love money, sex, and human praise.

3. Here are five ways to recognize a true teacher from a false one.

    1. Are they humble? (see verse 10)
    2. Do they model the qualities of a Christian as outlined in chapter 1?
    3. Do they encourage you to question them and read scripture for yourself?
    4. Do they mock parts of scripture or leave out sections they don't agree with from their sermons/messages?

5. Do they pull a verse from here and there but not show the way it lines up with all of scripture? Do they use it out of context to try to make a point?

Lord,

We have seen with our own eyes, or at least in the news, many examples of false teachers. They are a misrepresentation of you and your church. Please give us discernment when we listen to or read spiritual teachings and help us to be courageous to not follow the crowd. We want to teach our children to discern truth and falsehood. By your grace, may we be so in tune with your Word and so led by your Spirit we quickly recognize anything or anyone who is not of you. Please protect us and the lambs of your flock. In Jesus's name, amen.

Survival Tip #13

Let Her In

One day, my mom sent a young gal from church to my door on (what I thought was) the worst day possible. My house was a wreck. My one-month-old wasn't sleeping at all, and my body was still recovering. To be completely honest, I did not want company. When Mom called and said that Susie was coming, I was shamefully irritated that she sent her up the road to my house. It was an ugly, fleshly moment, and now, I don't know where I would be without that divine knock on my door.

Susie had a three-and-a-half-month-old, handsome boy in her arms, and she needed a place to use the bathroom and nurse him. You see, we live out in the country, and those places are few and far between. I put on my best smile and welcomed her into my disaster of a home. Susie sat down, nursed her baby, and chatted about how amazing motherhood had been and how many surprising lessons she had learned. I nodded in shock and eagerly watched her every move to see what I could learn from this happy new mom.

Then I'll never forget it. She laid her baby boy down on the floor next to my baby girl, and with sparkling, genuine eyes said, "Just look at them. Aren't they amazing? I mean to think that God lets us raise these precious babes. Look at their sweet faces. I just love being his mom. If only I could just hold him all day. He's amazing." She just kept going on and on about how amazing they are, and she said it with her entire being. You could hear it in her voice and see it in her eyes. As simple as that sounds, it is exactly what I needed to hear that day.

I loved my baby with all of my heart, and I was (and still am) fiercely protective of her, but that day I saw a true enjoyment in Susie's mothering that deeply impacted me. She was just as worn out and overwhelmed as I was, but she was choosing joy. It's still hard to explain, but something just clicked in that moment. I needed a fellow new momma in my life to learn from and share the journey alongside. God sent Susie. It took my own wise mom to see what I needed and get me to open that door, and I am so glad that I did. We are still very close friends today and it has been so wonderful to watch our babies grow up to become big kids and also good friends.

Let another new or newish mom in. You just never know what kind of friendship God has in store for both of you. Also, never underestimate the wisdom of your mom.

DAY 30

TODAY'S READING

2 Peter 2:16–19

1. I've often laughed while recalling the story of God giving a donkey the ability to speak (see Numbers 22). Here Peter reminds us God did that because the prophet Balaam had lost his mind. I hope that God never has to use a talking donkey to shut me up.

2. Take heart. The Lord will rescue His children, and He will deal with false teachers accordingly. Another check to know if you are following a false teacher is to see if your cup is being filled. Is your thirst being satisfied, or are you left longing and empty? God's Word quenches our thirst, satisfies us, and fills us. We feel refreshed and renewed after being with the Lord and being taught His truth.

3. More than once, Peter mentions that false teachers were given over to sensual passions and sexual sins. What does your church teach about sex? What does your church teach about women, men, and their roles within the family, church, and society? What do you believe? What does the Bible teach?

Let marriage be held in honor among all and let the marriage bed be undefiled. (Hebrews 13:4)

The husband should give to his wife her conjugal rights, and likewise the wife to her husband. For the wife does not have authority over her own body, but the husband does. Likewise, the husband does not have authority over his own body, but the wife does. (1 Corinthians 7:3–4)

Therefore, be imitators of God, as beloved children. And walk in love, as Christ loved us and gave himself up for us, a fragrant offering and sacrifice to God. But sexual immorality and all impurity or covetousness must not even be named among you, as is proper among saints. Let there be no filthiness nor foolish talk nor crude joking, which are out of place, but instead let there be thanksgiving. For you may be sure of this, that everyone who is sexually immoral or impure, or who is covetous (that is, an idolater), has no inheritance in the kingdom of Christ and God. (Ephesians 5:1–33)

Husbands love your wives, and do not be harsh with them. (Colossians 3:19)

Husbands, love your wives, as Christ loved the church and gave himself up for her.

(Ephesians 5:25)

Ice Rescue Mission

When it's cold, rainy, or super-hot outside, this activity is a win-win. It can be done in the bathtub, a plastic container, or outside in the sun to cool everyone off.

Supplies Needed
- large plastic bowl
- small plastic toys
- plastic tools, metal spoons, medicine syringes, eyedroppers, spray bottles, or anything that can be used to remove ice from the toys
- water
- freezer

Directions
1. Place toys inside bowl.
2. Fill bowl with water.
3. Place bowl in freezer for several hours.
4. When it is frozen solid, turn bowl upside down and let the dome-shaped ice mountain slide out into the container or onto the table.
5. Hand your kids the tools along with a small bowl of warm water and dramatically exclaim, "Your toys were caught in an ice storm and need rescued!" or, "Elsa froze your toys! Help them break free!"
6. Grab your favorite book or drink and relax. They will be good for at least a solid thirty minutes.

DAY 31

TODAY'S READING

2 Peter 2:20–22

1. It is better for them to never have heard the truth in the first place than to have the knowledge of whom Christ is and turn away from Him. We need to guard ourselves daily and to pray for those in leadership roles within the church. Pray for their souls. Pray for them to have eyes fixed on Christ, purity in their thinking and actions, humility as they study and teach, wisdom in their leading, correctness in their theology and doctrine, and that they would honor the Lord God in all they say and do.

The hiring process within our denomination makes my husband and me shudder. Pastors don't really know the kind of church family they are joining, and churches don't really know the kind of person they are hiring. It is based on a few interviews, a rehearsed sermon, and a meet and greet. Anyone can put on a good face for a few moments at a time. That's why we all must be filled daily with the Spirit through prayer, reading God's Word, and listening to His leading. The moment that we take our eyes off Him, we quickly sink like Peter walking on the water with his eyes fixed on Christ as told in the Gospels).

2. The phrase, "Returning to our own vomit," is used often when discussing addiction. The point in both instances is that apart from a genuine repentance and heart change, it will be a continuous cycle and become worse for the person than it was before. People can change, but it takes genuine, sorrowful repentance, accountability, clinging to God's Word, and uncovering any wounds that may have led to the behavior.

Even Christian counselors can be false teachers. True biblical counselors won't twist the Word of God to make you feel shame or condemnation. They also won't offer you Band-Aids, but they will walk with you through the healing journey and keep pointing you toward the hope of Christ.

Jesus,

Thank you for pastors and counselors who honor you and desire to teach biblical truth, love, and adoration of you. Thank you for the leaders who walk by your Spirit. They cry tears over the people who have been entrusted to their care and long to honor and glorify your name alone.

We always hear of the wolves, but we take the many shepherds who love you and long to see people walking by faith and in your joy for granted. Please bless these leaders mightily. They still make mistakes, but they grieve over those mistakes and strive to lead well for the good of the people and not for praise.

Please give us all discernment to know when a leader is for you and not themselves. You are the ultimate example, and we thank you for protecting, loving, guiding, and comforting us. We are never alone. We love you, too. Amen.

Survival Tip #14

Praying through Sleepless Nights

Pray Up and Stay Soft

Sleep depravity is real. I didn't trust myself on Amazon in the middle of the night and didn't have a brain function that was strong enough to read a novel or even blog articles after so little sleep for so many nights. However, I did have the strength to pray, and I did. My prayer life took off during that first year of our oldest child's life. I would pace the dining room all hours of the night, swaying, and praying while I held her in my arms.

Most of my prayers were for the many friends I had who were struggling with the pain of infertility. This kept me grateful in the darkness. We too had struggled with that pain, so I knew it all too well, and my heart ached for those friends because I knew they would give almost anything to be awake and pacing at 3 a.m. with their own baby in their arms. I lifted them in prayer to God night after night.

He is so gracious. He heard those prayers, and today, I give Him all glory and praise because those same gals are rocking their own babies. Some send their kids to preschool while one is homeschooling a kindergartner. Another has adopted her beautiful daughter. Their arms are no longer empty. Thank you, Jesus. Pray, sweet momma. He hears and cares.

Keep your heart soft. When you are that tired (maybe still healing from childbirth) and overwhelmed, it is so easy to become bitter.

You may be bitter at the baby who won't sleep or the God who just won't make the baby sleep. You may be bitter at your husband because you think that he should be more helpful or maybe less helpful in some cases. You may be bitter because he is sleeping. You may be bitter at those around you for not magically reading your mind. You may be bitter at the hospital staff for failing in big or small ways during such a critical time in both you and your baby's lives. You may be bitter with other moms on the Internet who have it all figured out or for their sleep advice that failed once again.

It can be so hard to release those unmet expectations, whether they are perceived or real, and choose grace and forgiveness. Ask Jesus to soften your heart, give you grace to forgive others and to give grace to others, and then move forward in releasing that hardness. Don't let it rob you of these precious days.

Here is the well-intended advice I received to get our first baby to sleep through the night:

- Nurse her every two hours.
- Don't nurse her during the night.
- Give her a bottle just before bed.
- Don't ever give her a bottle.
- Give her a soft toy or blanket to get attached to.
- Swaddle her tight but give her nothing that she can get attached to.
- Give her a pacifier to soothe her.
- Whatever you do, don't give her a pacifier or she will have nipple confusion.
- Let her cry it out, or else, she will have issues when she grows up.
- Never make a baby cry it out, or she will have issues when she grows up.
- Give her a little oatmeal in a bottle to fill her up.
- Babies should never have oatmeal as a filler.
- Use a sound machine.
- Don't use any noisemakers.
- Make sure that she is on her back.
- Keep her on her stomach to help her tummy settle.
- Sleep brings about more sleep, so make sure she takes good naps.
- Don't let her nap but wear her out well during the day.

- Lots of fresh air will do the trick.
- Keep her inside because she might have allergies.

I could go on and on. Maybe you can relate? We tried it all and now I can laugh about it. Seven years later, she sleeps through the night (mostly).

DAY 32

TODAY'S READING

2 Peter 3:1–8

1. As we have discussed before, every generation speaks as though it were the last one and that Jesus is coming at any minute. I used to roll my eyes at this, and then my husband said, "It's a good thing. It's good and right that every generation says that." He's right. It is good because we always should feel an urgency. I don't know about you, but I tend to procrastinate. If I don't feel an urgency, I don't get a lot done. However, if I truly remember that Jesus could come back at any moment and it is drawing nearer by the hour (which is true), I'm a lot more motivated to spread the news.

We should have one prayerful eye on those who do not yet believe and one eye to the sky eagerly awaiting His return. Those who mock His return will be in for a painful, gut-wrenching shock one day, and it may be very soon. My heart aches for them.

2. When people question the Lord's return or think they have it all figured out to the hour, verse 8 is a great reminder. The Lord is not constricted by time. It doesn't limit Him, and He does not operate by the clock. He is the beginning, the end, and already in both places.

3. I love that Peter said, "beloved," which refers to the church. People were alarmed and worried about the false teachers, and they may have even been tempted to believe the doubting and scoffing. Instead of saying, "You idiot, of course they aren't telling the truth," he said, "Remember, beloved." May we have the same gentleness for those who doubt and struggle and even for our own children as they also learn and grow.

For My thoughts are not your thoughts, neither are your ways My ways, declares the Lord. "As the heavens are higher than the earth, so are My ways higher than your ways and My thoughts than your thoughts." (Isaiah 55:8–9)

Nursing Home Visits

During the first six years of parenting littles, my grandma Mary Elizabeth was in the nursing home. Packing up a preschooler, toddler, and a baby to visit a nursing home can be quite a challenge. We never knew if Grandma would be awake or feel up to company and if the children would be at their best for a visit. When Grandma was awake and felt up to it, it was a precious and sweet time together for her, me, and our children.

It is good for children to be with the elderly. It is good for the elderly to be with children. Grandma was always worth the effort, even when she wasn't awake, wasn't up to the visit, didn't know me, or didn't recognize the children. Our entire family took turns visiting to help make her feel loved, and making someone feel loved is always worth the effort. She appreciated the company and distraction. When she did remember who I was, she would always tell me, "I love you. Don't you forget it." I never have and never will.

Here are a few suggestions to help make the visits as smooth as possible if you find yourself in a similar position.

1. If they are physically able and allowed to go for a drive, it is an easy way to visit and also keep the kids entertained.
2. Keep a small container of toys packed in the closet in his/her room. My parents did this for us and it helped so much. While you visit, the kids can play with the special toys that are only at grandmas. Grandparents love to watch them play.
3. Try to schedule your visits right after nap time.
4. Pick up Happy Meals or cookies at a drive-through and bring them with you. Don't forget some ice cream for Grandpa.
5. Bring a book or the Bible and read to your children and grandparent.
6. Put a guest book at the entrance to the room so that even if he or she is asleep or not up for visits, you can log that you came. Your kids can leave a note too.
7. Have your children make cards and posters to brighten the room.
8. Talk often about Grandma at home so that when you go for a visit, the children remember her and aren't afraid.

9. Have the children hang and fill a bird feeder outside the window or plant flowers (if it's okay with the staff).

10. Take lots of pictures of the kids with their great-grandparents or elderly friends. They will be treasured forever.

DAY 33

TODAY'S READING

2 Peter 3:9

1. Have you ever asked Jesus to return and be done with it? I have. I have actually begged for Him to come back just to end the heartache and brokenness. I've also prayed it out of fear for what our children will experience in life. In my mind, it would be so much easier and better for us if Jesus would just come back today. However, in verse 9, He reminds us of His patience. He is giving everyone an opportunity to repent and be ready. What a good and gracious God He is.

2. So does it mean that God has called everyone but not everyone will repent? Yes. However, those who desire faith will have it. We pray daily for the salvation of our children, knowing that salvation comes from the Lord. Ephesians 2:8–9 says, "For by grace you have been saved through faith, and this is not your own doing; it is the gift of God, not a result of works, so that no one may boast."

3. If the Lord comes back today, what's your relationship status with Him?

4. Whom do you want to share Jesus with before He returns? Make a list and begin asking God to work in their hearts and give them opportunities to hear the gospel. He may use you in that process, so be ready. Remember, a mother's mission field begins at home.

Survival Tip #15

Shopping with Littles

When I venture out with the kiddos, there is a huge difference in their behavior based on whether or not I have set the expectations for all of us. For myself, I prepare for crazy and pray up. I ask God to protect us, give me patience and wisdom, help me to enjoy my kids, and make peaceful, calm decisions. For the children, I ask them to each bring one toy and one snack for the outing. Once we pull into the parking spot, I set the tone.

1. Use inside voices so we don't distract others.
2. Walk, and not run so we respect the store and others.
3. Stay right beside mommy so that we do not get lost or taken by a stranger.
4. Look with their eyes and not with their hands.
5. Show me what they like by pointing or commenting, but they do not ask for things.

When I forget to do this, I notice immediately, and we spend the rest of the time scrambling. It's rough. I also expect them to be worn out and bored in the checkout line (They are kids after all), which is why I often also pack fruit snacks or suckers. Those have really pulled us through during the last fifteen minutes.

After one slightly rough store experience we were headed to the van and my sweet middle child's shoe fell off in the middle of the parking lot. I quickly pulled her back to me as she was trying to go after her shoe while a car was backing out and at that exact moment our watermelon fell off the cart and began rolling down the hill between cars. Praise God for the amazing woman who chased it down and kindly asked, "Is this your melon?" She laughed, looked at my full hands and told me she remembered those days. May God bless her richly.

DAY 34

TODAY'S READING

2 Peter 3:10

We are taking these verses in small chunks because they are heavy.

1. How will the day of the Lord come? It will come like a thief. Thieves appear when we least expect it. We don't know when Jesus is coming either. If we did, we would probably clean up our acts quickly the day before He was to arrive. It's like when your mom left you a list of things to do before she got back, and you did them all as quickly as possible, ten minutes before her expected arrival time. If we would have spent more time on each task, putting effort and care into it, and shown her more honor and respect, it would probably have helped the relationship.

It's the same with Jesus. Our relationship with Him isn't about checking things off the list before He gets back, or we die. It's about honoring, showing love and devotion, and worshipping Him through the journey. He plans to use us to disciple others and bless us as His children. While we eagerly await His return, our actions show Him love, bring Him glory, and strengthen our relationship with Him.

2. What did Peter mention about the arrival of Jesus? He didn't mention much. He focused on the burning up of the heavens and the earth and all the works done on the earth. His point was that everything the false teachers cared about would burn up and be destroyed in the end: fame, money, their bodies, their treasures—all of it.

That's a good reminder for us as well. What are we storing up as treasures here on earth? What teachings do we pay the most attention to? Are we excited to study the Word of God and glean wisdom from our pastors and solid biblical teachers? Would we rather have our ears tickled and avoid hard topics?

Lord God,

You are holy and mighty. In the end, nothing will stand except your church. You are coming back, and we eagerly await your arrival. May we have one eye looking to the sky and one eye to the work that you have prepared for us today. Please use us to further your kingdom while there is still time. Please help us to show and teach our children the things that really matter in eternity. May we enjoy earthly blessings and be grateful for them, but may we invest and commit to our relationship with, our love of, our knowledge of, and our worship of you. You alone are worthy. We love you. Amen.

Mommy's Power Smoothie

Ingredients

- 1 frozen banana
- 1 cup coffee
- 3 tablespoons flavored creamer (I prefer peppermint mocha)
- 1 Scoop protein powder or Carnation Breakfast Essentials Nutritional Drink Mix
- handful of ice

Preparation

Blend all ingredients together. If too thick, add a little water or milk. If too runny, add more ice or a little ice cream.

The Perfect Playdate Lunch for Kids

Our sweet middle child goes with the flow really well usually. I hear that's a typical middle-child thing. Her favorite meal to make almost by herself is a peanut butter and honey sandwich (with the crust removed of course).

Ingredients

- 2 slices of bread
- Jif Peanut Butter
- honey (We prefer local honey from our niece. It's amazing.)

- 1 banana to serve on the side
- a handful of veggie straws or a bag of Goldfish crackers
- juice bag or box

It's perfect for a park date because you don't have to worry about anything melting or going bad.

DAY 35

TODAY'S READING

2 Peter 3:11–12

1. Here Peter explained the therefore to remind us what it is "there for". If heaven and earth will melt away, how should we live? What occupies our minds and energy? Is it our bodies, appearance, status at work, or approval ratings with other moms? What are we teaching our kids? Are we teaching them that jobs, school, and sports are more important than the Church and Jesus? It all burns up in the end. Only one thing remains: our position before Christ.

2. Peter flat-out asked, "What manner of persons are we to be?" I once read somewhere that we need to write down who we want to be and be that person. In some cases, I think that is a good goal-oriented approach, and it can be very helpful. In other case, it goes much deeper, and counseling, mentoring, and guidance may need to take place in order to become who you want to be. There is no shame in seeing a counselor. We live in a broken world, and we all have baggage. I'm so thankful for the counselors, mentors, and teachers who have poured into my life.

3. As we discussed earlier in this letter (1:3), God has given us all we need for life and godliness. Ask Him for wisdom, help, strength, and grace to live according to His will and His best for your life so that you may honor and glorify Him and best serve the kingdom. We have the Holy Spirit as our helper. We are not alone. Ask His Spirit to fill you today.

Our Family Verse

Be joyful in hope, patient in affliction, faithful in prayer. (Romans 12:12)

We have this as our family verse and it hangs on the wall in our kitchen. It has been the best heart check for all of us at just the right moments. It has put my heart at ease through many rocky days and stressful, trying times.

Do you have a family verse? If not, I would encourage you to pray about it and be on the lookout for a verse that truly speaks to you and your husband. If he isn't into it, that's okay. Go ahead and hang it on the wall or your fridge and pray for it to minister to your family in ways that you'll never expect. God's Word is powerful.

DAY 36

TODAY'S READING

2 Peter 3:13

There will be a new heaven and a new earth.

Lord,

We can't even begin to wrap our minds around what the new heaven and the new earth will look like or how beautiful life will be at that point for your children. "Where righteousness dwells," tells me there will be no sin. Halleluiah! We are so thankful that we can look forward to an eternity without sin, brokenness, death, and sickness. Lord God, thank you for the hope of our future.

This world is not our home. Please remind us of that every time we get caught up and overwhelmed by the stress and chaos around us. We are just passing through this world. I pray that we will leave a mark on it that brings glory to your name and that you will use us to further the gospel while we are here. May we raise up arrows (our children), and may they continue the mission until you arrive. Thank you for your many graces that carry us through each day and bring smiles to our faces.

We love you. Amen.

Hope: Waiting with Great Expectation

As followers of Christ who have a relationship with Him and not only a religion, we have so much to look forward to. Today, I just want to encourage you and help set our hearts and minds on the hope that lies before us. Here are some other verses in the Bible that talk about the new heaven and earth.

Now I saw a new heaven and a new earth, for the first heaven and the first earth had passed away. Also, there was no more sea. Then I, John, saw the holy city, New Jerusalem, coming down out of heaven from God, prepared as a bride adorned for her husband. And I heard a loud voice from heaven saying, "Behold, the tabernacle of God is with men, and He will dwell with them, and they shall be His people. God Himself will be with them and be their God. And God will wipe away every tear from their eyes; there shall be no more death, nor sorrow, nor crying. There shall be no more pain, for the former things have passed away." Then He who sat on the throne said, "Behold, I make all things new." And He said to me, "Write, for these words are true and faithful." **(Revelation 21:1–5)**

The construction of its wall was of jasper; and the city was pure gold, like clear glass.

(Revelation 21:18)

The twelve gates were twelve pearls: each individual gate was of one pearl. And the street of the city was pure gold, like transparent glass. **(Revelation 21:21)**

For behold, I create new heavens and a new earth; and the former shall not be remembered or come to mind. But be glad and rejoice forever in what I create; for behold, I create Jerusalem as a rejoicing, and her people a joy. I will rejoice in Jerusalem, and joy in My people; the voice of weeping shall no longer be heard in her, nor the voice of crying. **(Isaiah 65:17–19)**

Yes, all kings shall fall down before Him; all nations shall serve Him. **(Psalm 72:11)**

In His days the righteous shall flourish, and abundance of peace, until the moon is no more. **(Psalm 72:7)**

The wolf also shall dwell with the lamb, the leopard shall lie down with the young goat, the calf and the young lion and the fatling together; and a little child shall lead them. The cow and the bear shall graze; their young ones shall lie down together; and the lion shall eat straw like the ox. The nursing child shall play by the cobra's hole, and the weaned child shall put his hand in the viper's den. They shall not hurt nor destroy in all My holy mountain, for the earth shall be full of the knowledge of the Lord as the waters cover the sea. **(Isaiah 11:6–9)**

"For as the new heavens and the new earth which I will make shall remain before Me," says the Lord, "So shall your descendants and your name remain." **(Isaiah 66:22)**

Thank you, Lord.

The Gift of the Mom Brain

After we had some electrical damage, an older man came to work on our home, and I couldn't remember some vital information to help him do his job well (something about where to shut off the power so that he wouldn't get electrocuted—details). I laughed, embarrassed, and chalked it up to having a mom brain.

He turned and said the following unforgettable words: "Ma'am, a mom brain is a gift. Don't ever wish you didn't have it. It's your mom brain that helps you protect, feed, nourish, and care for those young'uns. Without it, you wouldn't be a good mom. It's a good thing you have a mom brain."

He had no idea the impact that he made on me that day. My brain may tell me to put the cereal box in the fridge sometimes, but it also tells me how to care for my sick baby in the night and helps me juggle my kids' many needs every second of the day. Thank you, God, for my mom brain.

Come to me, all who labor and are heavy laden, and I will give you rest. Take my yoke upon you, and learn from me, for I am gentle and lowly in heart, and you will find rest for your souls. For my yoke is easy, and my burden is light. (Matthew 11:28–30)

DAY 37

TODAY'S READING

2 Peter 3:14

1. Therefore—again, we have to ask. "What's the therefore *there for*?" The verse just prior to this says that we are waiting according to His promise, for the new earth, in which righteousness dwells. While we are waiting for the new heaven and earth, what are we supposed to do?

2. Wait a minute. It says without spot or blemish. Does it mean that we have to be sinless when He returns? Will we have reached perfection? Let's look at it in context. Just a few weeks ago in 1 Peter, we read that we are to be holy like a lamb without spot or blemish because of the precious blood of Christ. Does God make a person blameless by Jesus's blood or do we work to be blameless? The answer is not either/or but both/and.

We are not capable of being free from sin on our own (see Romans 1:18–3:18). God saves us, changes our hearts, and cleanses us by the blood of the perfect, spotless Lamb, Jesus, His mercy, and His grace. Peter wrote these letters to believers: those who had already been washed by the blood of Christ and were forgiven. Once we have received that grace and forgiveness, as believers, we have to (as Paul says in Philippians 2:12) work out our salvation. We respond and display our position in Christ by continually growing, striving, and following His teachings.

We all have room for more growth. We won't reach true perfection or peace until Christ returns, but we are urged to remain diligent in honoring, loving, and seeking Him and growing in our faith. If we do not desire this, we must do some serious soul-searching to determine where we stand before Christ. Are you truly His? Have you experienced Him? Pray. Ask the tough questions, and stay diligent. Peace will be yours if you do.

Safety Tips for Children

Too many children and women are forced into sex trafficking each year. One is too many. Heartbreakingly, it is estimated that 199,000 incidents occur within the United States every year involving some degree of human trafficking (sex trafficking, child pornography, etc.) according to the World Population Review.

This is the greatest fear I struggle with regarding our children, and I continually have to hand it and them over to the Lord. They are His. He has also made me a mama bear, and He has called me to do my best to protect and nurture them in this world. Thankfully, He didn't ask me to do this alone. He is with us, and He has given us wisdom, tools, and an ever-growing network of people to help in this specific area. From the materials I have read, the trained people I have spoken to, and the experiences we have had, here is a list of safety tips I've compiled.

Private

Even as a toddler, begin teaching children the names of their private areas (technical names and not nicknames) and explaining that they are private. No one touches or asks to see them—not a cousin, sibling, uncle, or friend. If it's a doctor, Mommy or Daddy must also be in the room.

What If?

If someone asks or tries, your child is to yell, "No!" Then he or she should run to Mommy and tell what happened. Assure your child that he or she will *not* be in trouble and Mommy will help them.

No Secrets

We tell our kids that secrets are never okay. Surprises for a birthday, Christmas, or something similar are acceptable, but secrets are not allowed in our family. They can hurt someone very seriously. If someone asks them to keep a secret, they are to tell Mommy or Daddy right away. Again, they will not get in trouble. I remind my children often that they can tell me anything.

Good

We teach them that their bodies are beautiful, good, and designed by God and they have nothing to be ashamed of but they are also special, to be kept special, and to be treated honorably. This is the reason that no one is allowed to photograph their private areas and they are not to see pictures of other people's private areas. If they do, they are to tell Mommy or Daddy. If they talk to us about it, they will not be in trouble.

Accountability

Our children will not be given any devices where they can access social media or the Internet while alone until they are teenagers, and even then, they will have strict restrictions and accountability. We have been told that giving your child an unfiltered phone or computer is like putting a pile of *Playboy* magazines in their closets for them to stumble on. Children and teenagers do not have the maturity (no matter how awesome you think your kid is) to handle the pressure, temptation, and sensuality of this world. It is our responsibility to protect and train them in these ways before they leave the shelter of our homes. We use Covenant Eyes in our home for Internet accountability and filtering.

Sex Education

Christian parents simply cannot leave sex education up to the school. The government does not hold the same values and worldview. Please start this at home and teach a solid, biblical foundation. We are using the God's Design for Sex series, which is available on Amazon. It covers just the right amount, for the right age and it is parent led.

Apps

Some apps are used by sex traffickers to manipulate and trick your children. Some but not all include Snapchat, Whisper, Kik Messenger, TikTok, and Houseparty—no joke. (www.familyeducation.com)

Shopping

While shopping, keep your head up, eyes alert, and phone handy. Some moms prefer to have a concealed-carry permit. I will say that I have had some uncomfortable moments. I'm thankful that I was on alert. Train your kids to stay right beside you. Teach them to scream and kick if anyone grabs them and that it's okay if you seem a little rude to the overfriendly stranger. Believe it or not, I had a handful of complete strangers ask if they could hold my baby for me while I was out shopping during our eldest child's first year of life. I answered, "Nope!" They were probably harmless, but it is never worth the risk.

Lost

Before your child gets lost like mine did once, teach them to look for a mommy with kids or a grandma. Our daughters are very shy and afraid of men who are outside of our family. I've read that finding a store manager can be scary and difficult (a lot of people wear uniforms these days), but if they can look for a mommy with kids, those people are usually the safest bet. Moms and grandmas also show great empathy, and they will be protective. My daughter couldn't find a mommy, but she found a grandma, and that lady kept her close and led her straight to the intercom so she could find me. Also, make sure that they can say your name and your phone number if they are old enough. Many parents teach their kids to stay where they are, but a scared child all alone can also become easy prey.

Pray

Lastly but most importantly, pray up. God alone can protect our children better than a gun, all of the safety training in the world, and even our mama bears' instincts. Nothing is fool proof in this depraved and broken world. Cover them in prayer and know that fear feeds the enemy.

Fear not, for I am with you; be not dismayed, for I am your God; I will strengthen you, I will help you, I will uphold you with my righteous right hand. (Isaiah 41:10)

DAY 38

TODAY'S READING

2 Peter 3:15–16

1. Sometimes, we may wonder why the Lord is waiting so long to return. When we look at the destruction and heartache around us, it is hard to wait. Peter said we should count the patience of the Lord as what? We are to count it as salvation. He is mighty to save. Remember that He wants to give everyone an opportunity. I'm so grateful that every day, thousands more people hear the gospel and believe. Thank you, God, for being patient.

2. Paul also wrote about the salvation of the Lord, followers of Christ living blameless lives, and being on guard against false teachers. We will look at some of those verses, but first, I want us to note the way that Peter honored and lifted up Paul. It's so easy for us to pick and choose which verses and segments of scripture we like and then dismiss the rest.

Paul had some strong words and language in his letters (see Romans, 1 and 2 Corinthians, Galatians, Ephesians, Philippians, Colossians, 1 and 2 Thessalonians, Philemon, Titus, and 1 and 2 Timothy). However, they are included in the Bible, inspired by the Holy Spirit, and for our good. They are life giving. I have learned so much about marriage, parenting, teaching, joy, patience, love, grace, salvation, serving others, and so on through his letters. I would encourage you to dive into them after reading the gospels if you never have before. As always, ask the Holy Spirit for understanding, learning, and faith as you read His Word.

Put on then, as God's chosen ones, holy and beloved, compassionate hearts, kindness, humility, meekness, and patience, bearing with one another and, if one has a complaint against another, forgiving each other; as the Lord has forgiven you, so you also must forgive.

(Colossians 3:12–13)

Who saved us and called us to a holy calling, not because of our works but because of his own purpose and grace, which he gave us in Christ Jesus before the ages began. (2 Timothy 1:9)

For the grace of God has appeared, bringing salvation for all people, training us to renounce ungodliness and worldly passions, and to live self-controlled, upright, and godly lives in the present age. (Titus 2:11–12)

Entitlement

How do you know if your kids feel entitled? I think all kids experience this to a degree, simply because they are children and they do not have a full understanding of what is involved in providing essentials and nonessentials for them. My husband's professor shared a valuable tip on knowing when your kids have crossed the line and gone into unhealthy entitlement. When you turn off the TV or take away a privilege, what happens? A little disappointment may be acceptable, but are there fits being thrown? Does whining ensue? Are they at a loss of what to do next? Are you met with eye-rolling and bad attitudes? Those are your signs.

We often use this gauge in our home. If they have watched enough TV, I give a gentle warning that it will need to be turned off after that episode or movie, and if they whine, cry, or have a bad attitude once the screen goes black, I know they are encroaching on the realm of entitlement. I'll let them know they need to be grateful for the screen time they had, their behavior is unacceptable, and they will have no more screen time for the remainder of the day or week (depending upon the severity of their actions). This is usually all it takes for a more grateful attitude to emerge. The next time it is turned off, they tend to remember to practice self-control and to be thankful.

At dinner, we sometimes talk about the difference between needs and wants. Wants are privileges, and needs are what we provide as good parents. Having nice clothes is a privilege, so let's take care of them and hang them up. Having toys is a privilege, so let's be responsible and put them away. Playing sports is a privilege, so let's learn well and work hard.

I also try to take note of the way that they ask for more to drink, toys, or snacks. Are they remembering their manners? Are they saying, "Thank you," for the request when it is met? Are they saying, "Thank you," to Daddy when he takes us out to dinner or buys us new clothes? My mom was so good about reminding us to run and tell my dad, "Thank you," when we got home from going shopping.

This is also a good check for my own heart. Am I remembering to thank God when a prayer is answered the way I asked it to be? Am I expressing gratitude in my worship to Him? Adults can be just as guilty of entitlement. It hits me like a brick sometimes.

"With great privilege comes great responsibility." -Anonymous

DAY 39

TODAY'S READING

2 Peter 3:17

1. What do we know beforehand? We now know the ignorant twist scripture and false teachers and prophets are speaking lies around us. We also know Christ is coming back. We know He is patient and gracious and giving us all a chance to be ready.

2. This was his final written warning in a letter before his death. What did Peter choose to write about to the church? He warned against following lawless people and losing our stability. Who are you following? Who has the greatest influence over your life? What or who is filling your cup daily? Yeshua is calling. Run to His open arms in prayer, and you will find Him faithful.

Breakfast Pizza

The only way my youngest kiddo will eat eggs is by scrambling them and putting them on pizza with lots of cheese. It's an easy favorite, and it warms up nicely as a leftover on a rushed morning.

Ingredients

- your favorite pizza crust (Jiffy is an easy mix)
- Velveeta cheese sauce
- scrambled eggs
- sausage or hamburger crumbles (diced ham also works)
- shredded cheese
- salt and pepper to taste

Directions

1. Mix up your crust and press it into a circle.
2. Spread cheese sauce in thin layer on top of the crust.
3. Top with scrambled eggs, meat, and shredded cheese.
4. Sprinkle a little salt and pepper on top.
5. Bake at 400 degrees for 20 minutes.

DAY 40

TODAY'S READING

2 Peter 3:18

1. These are Peter's final written words to the church. I want to encourage you, friend. By choosing to study these letters with me for even ten minutes a day, you have actively been growing in the grace and knowledge of Jesus. You have learned more about what it looks like to be a Christ follower. You have learned more about the heart of God and His people. I pray that the Spirit will remind you of these truths at just the right moments. How do you plan to continue your growth?

2. To God be the glory both now and forever. We do not grow in knowledge for our own glory. We do not study and learn so we can simply know Bible facts, impress others, or earn our way to heaven. We grow in grace and knowledge for the glory of God alone. He alone is worthy, and we owe it all to Him. Not living for ourselves or the praise of others should be freeing. We live for a gracious, loving, and merciful Savior, who has already made us righteous so we can grow and find peace in Him.

3. In what ways have you grown while doing this study? In what areas would you like to continue your growth specifically?

Lord Jesus,

Thank you for this time to study the letters of Peter. Thank you for Peter's life and the sacrifice he made for the church. Thank you for speaking through him in ways that still teach, encourage, and convict us today. Thank you for not giving up on us and causing us to grow in grace and knowledge. I pray they would balance one another.

Please give us a hunger and desire to continue to grow and that we will not be satisfied with imitation milk. May we have the courage to open our Bibles daily and glean from your teaching, truth, wisdom, and life-giving food for our souls. Please protect us from false teaching and the snares of the evil one.

May we be as wise as serpents and as gentle as doves. I pray that our cups would be so full of godliness, hope, joy, peace, patience, kindness, gentleness, and self-control that when our kids knock them over, they are showered in your love and the fruits of our being with you and walking by your Spirit. May they see and experience you in us. Thank you, Lord. Amen.

Humility in Motherhood

When Ryan and I got married, I was shocked by my own selfishness. It was hard to go from living on my own to constantly checking in with another person, considering their needs before my own, and striving to love them well while sharing the same roof.

Marriage has shown me my selfishness, and parenthood has shown me my pride. I didn't realize how prideful I was until I became a mom. If my kids are going to throw a fit or disobey, it will most likely be in public or in front of family. If my house is going to look like a tornado blew through it, it will be on a day when someone stops by or an emergency happens. If I'm going to burn supper or forget the seasoning, it will be when company is here. If I for one second think that I've got something figured out when it comes to motherhood, it all instantly changes, and I'm utterly stumped the next minute.

It's hard and it's humbling. All I can do is give my best. God knows. He sees, and He provides. When the days are extra-long and I fall flat on my face more than once, I have to remember that God loves these kids even more than I do, and He also loves me.

Yet she will be saved through childbearing—if they continue in faith and love and holiness, with self-control. (1 Timothy 2:15)

The act of raising a child is sanctifying. We become more like Christ when we die to ourselves, kill our pride, lay down our lives for our children, love when it's easier not to, discipline with self-control and kindness, and press in, even though it would be easier to run. It is worth it. They are worth it. He is worth it.

An older song called "All in All" written by Dennis Jernigan, has blessed my children and me during rough days. I have sung it to them thousands of times, and they still request it when they are sad, hurt, or overly tired. I hope it blesses you as well. Feel free to check it out on YouTube and have a good cry.

DAY 41

TODAY'S READING

John 1:1–2

1. Yes, we have finished 1 and 2 Peter. However, I didn't want that to be the end. I want to encourage and spur you on to further study the Word. My prayer is that you have now tasted and seen your need for and ability to receive the Word of God and to fill your cup with it daily. Remember, it only takes ten minutes a day (if that's all you have). Read, pray, and grow. If you don't have anything else lined up, you might want to start with the book of John next? It is full of wisdom, Jesus's life story, and hope. After all, John was the *beloved* disciple, as Jesus called him. How cool is that?

2. In the beginning, what was there? The Word was there. Who was the Word? Jesus was the Word.

3. Here are some tips for reading the Bible. Start by asking God to speak to you through His Word and to help you understand it. Pay close attention to repetitive words and phrases because they are usually important. Ask what the therefore is there for. Find out who the author of the book was and what life was like when it was written. Listen carefully for the Holy Spirit, as He might be encouraging, convicting, or teaching you something you need to hear right now. Write down a key verse that stood out to you, and don't be afraid to ask questions. Study Bibles are really helpful.

4. Enjoy learning more from the Word. Our Savior is waiting.

With love and blessings, Kara

WITH ADMIRATION

Throughout this book, I have mentioned many women God graciously placed in my life. They are women whom I deeply respect, and they deserve an entire page each, if I could do so. They all play a major role in my village. There are a few other women whom I didn't get to mention yet, and I admire them with everything in me. Allow me to share a little about these incredible ladies, and you'll see the reason that neither I nor this book would be complete without them.

Sharon (Aunt Dobby) is like a sister to me. We have ridden many waves together, and it feels like I have known her my entire life, although God didn't have our paths cross until 2003. Sharon is not a mother in the traditional sense, but she is in every other sense of the word and meaning. This amazing woman has taken many troubled teens under her wing and poured her heart into them. She loves and cares for her nieces and nephews as if they were her own, even to the point of housing them while they attend college. She has helped cover expenses for adoptions, and she encourages every mom that she knows through praise, loving on their kids, treating them to fun places, and serving as a listening ear when the momma is stressed.

She doesn't have children herself, but that hasn't stopped her from being the loudest fan for every mom in her circle. For over forty years, she has served at a Christian camp for kids, and she has given her all to this camp so that children of all ages can know Jesus. God has used her to influence more children and families than we will ever know this side of heaven. She's an amazing "mom," sister, and friend to many. I just hope that she sees it.

Another beloved friend is Naomi. Naomi is a single mom but not by choice. She has been through the worst years of her life but remained steady and hopeful for those two handsome sons that she is raising. Her boys never hear her speak an ill-intentioned word about their father. She has humbly expressed to me her acknowledgement of the importance of their relationship with their dad and that she doesn't want to hinder them from it. Their daddy doesn't believe in Jesus, and those boys pray often for his salvation. Naomi's tender heart, devotion, and faithfulness to God's will for her life blows me away. She has walked through the fire, and God has never left her side. He is redeeming her life. I'm so excited for the next chapter of her story.

My Aunt Rhonda is one of the strongest people I know. Aunt Rhonda has served our country as the wife of a US Airforce serviceman. They have moved a lot. Her husband has had many stressful and very honorable roles involving military secrets, which he couldn't even share with his own wife. She raised four amazing kids (my favorite first cousins) far away from home and family.

When her youngest two (twin girls) were just babies, she was diagnosed with stage-IV ovarian cancer and fought hard. It was one military plane ride after another for treatment. However, God used those treatments and mercifully healed her. She has lived to hold her beautiful grandbabies.

Their family has faced many other battles, but they have done it together. By God's grace, she has remained faithful. Her twin daughters are incredible mommas themselves. Her son is a committed father. Her beautiful middle child is one of the most fun, devoted aunties, and teachers I know. I only wish that we all lived closer.

Printed in the United States
by Baker & Taylor Publisher Services